Topanga Beach

Topanga Beach

A HISTORY

1820s–1920s

Pablo Capra

Los Angeles, CA
2020

BRASS TACKS PRESS
Los Angeles, CA
brasstackspress@yahoo.com
www.brasstackspress.com

Eighth Edition, August 2025

These chapters were first published in Topanga's
Messenger Mountain News between 2018–2020

ISBN 978-0-9820140-4-2

Contents

Acknowledgments

Thank you to the *Messenger Mountain News* for first publishing these chapters between 2018-2020.

Thank you to the Topanga Historical Society for their support.

Thank you to Diane Belle James for copy editing.

Thank you to the many people who helped me research this history, especially…

Allison-Claire Acker	Acker Archive
Susan Chasen	*Topanga Messenger* editor, 2001–2003
Samuel Fort	*Cult of the Great Eleven* author
Dr. Alison Rose Jefferson	*Living the California Dream* author
Dr. John R. Johnson	Anthropologist
Dr. Laura Jones	Archaeologist
Justina Judge-Stevenson	Laura Way relative
Dr. Chester King	Anthropologist
Ami Kirby	Topanga Historical Society
The Larronde Family	Pedro and Gladys Larronde relatives
Beverly Spence Kirkpatrick	William and Florence Spence relative
The Sykes Family	Clayton and Ina Rust relatives
Barbara Tejada	Archaeologist
Larry Telles	*Helen Gibson: Silent Serial Queen* author
Jataun Valentine	Arthur and Charlotte Valentine relative
Randy Young	Pacific Palisades Historical Society

Thank you to anyone who can contribute more to this history. Please contact me at brasstackspress@yahoo.com.

CHAPTER I

Native Americans of Topanga Beach

> For years it has been known that a number of Indian bones were buried all along the bluffs by the sea. Occasionally after a high tide, relics... are to be seen, the high water having removed the covering of earth and exposed them to crumble in the air.
>
> —"Skeletons and Skulls of Warriors Are Excavated"
> *Los Angeles Times*, 1910-07-19

On June 27, 1910, a class of Stanford University students from the Mining Department and their Geology professor John Roy "Billie" Pemberton (1884-1968) pitched tents at Topanga Beach, camping, or glamping, with Japanese cooks and "everything required for [their] convenience."

Professor Pemberton, just 25 years old, had recently been a Stanford student himself. Attractive and athletic, he was a football player, rower, and sailor. He was also greatly interested in birds, having spent his youth studying them in what's now known as MacArthur Park, and would go on to publish many articles on Ornithology. He moved to San Francisco in his teens, and experienced the deadliest earthquake in US history there in 1906. Before deciding on a career in Geology, he seriously considered becoming a professional boxer.

He and his students, "clad in khaki suits, wearing sombreros, and with several weeks' growth of beard," were supposed to be studying oil formations in the rocks, but by mid-July they were digging up Native American graves at Topanga Beach and in Temescal Canyon.

At Topanga Beach, they discovered 34 skeletons, all of which appeared to have been buried at the same time. Men and women, young and old, were buried close together, but predominant were older men, identified by their worn-down teeth. Other reports said that pieces of over 100 skeletons had been found, and speculated that 300 skeletons would be revealed when the mound was fully excavated.

At least one of the skulls had an arrowhead embedded in it. Others were crushed. A Stanford Archaeology class came to assist, and conjectured that the graves were evidence of a massacre that had occurred around the year 1200.

Strangely, the class reported that the skeletons "were almost dwarfs in size," and listed other abnormalities.

> The brow is almost totally lacking, rising from the line of the eyebrows only three-quarters of an inch, and the top of the head being almost flat.... [The nose] projects horizontally, hornlike, and with no resemblance to the human nose. A spirit level laid from the top of the head to the tip of the nose would show but a slight inclination.
>
> These queer tribesmen had bulging heads in the rear and unusually heavy jaw bones, due probably to their diet of clams and other shell fish, the shells of which they crushed between their teeth.
>
> —"Unheard of Race," *Marion County Progress*, 1910-11-12

> Another of the skulls had horns, which protruded from near the front of the ear cavity and encircled the head. These horns, which were two or three inches in length, were apparently of the same bone composition as the skulls and had evidently been a part of them; but they were so slender and mellow with age that at the first handling after exposure to the air the horns became separated from the skull.
>
> —"Will They Be Interpreted?" *Los Angeles Times*, 1911-02-05

Artifacts discovered in the mound included flint arrowheads, deer-bone whistles, shell ornaments in the shape of fish and animals, necklace beads, stone discs, mortars, and small cups with holes on either side near the top. One newspaper reported that the artifacts were unlike anything known from the surrounding Native Americans (for example, flint isn't found in the area, and "other articles had been made of stone that is not found in this part of the world"). Another reported that large rocks, cut into the shapes of "spinning tops," resembled the fishing lures of Channel Islands Natives.

When the class returned to Stanford, credit for their discovery was suddenly claimed by a miner and self-styled "amateur archaeologist" named William Wills Coolbaugh (1839-1912), who was homesteading at Topanga Beach in a cabin he called Jack Rabbit Lodge.

Coolbaugh said he'd been "prospecting along the beach when he came upon a six acre flat, at the delta of the Topango," that had a 40′ x 100′ mound of darker soil on it. The mound was 5-8′ high and overgrown. Digging into it, he noticed a protective layer of boulders, then ashes and tiny seashells, and finally whale bones covering 44 skeletons with their knees bound to their chests.

Coolbaugh left the skeletons "lying visible in their tombs" as a macabre attraction, charging tourists 25 cents to see them. By August 1910, he had begun selling artifacts to Professor Ira M. Buell (1849-1931) of Beloit College, Wisconsin, including a 4″ arrowhead for $10. The college still has over a dozen stone tools from the site in its collection.

Professor Buell, "The Bone Man," had come to Los Angeles earlier that year to collect bones from the La Brea Tar Pits. In July, his wife Lillian (b.1858), an artist and art teacher, had an exhibition of her drawings in the parlor of the Witherow Hotel on Ocean Ave. *The Daily Outlook* wrote, "She has been sketching around Santa Monica and Topanga for four months and has many of our most interesting views." It seems natural that she would have drawn Coolbaugh's homestead or the mound.

When Professor Buell inspected the Topanga Beach skeletons, he also noted their abnormalities. He conjectured that the burials had taken place 500-1,000 years ago.

Interestingly, he observed that some of the bones were buried in a rotting wooden box, and concluded that they had been dug up before and reburied. On the ground nearby, he found evidence of lodge sites.

At Coolbaugh's request, the Smithsonian Institute came to study the mound, but no information could be found about their research.

Enjoying the publicity, Coolbaugh offered up many of his own conjectures. He imaginatively linked the graves to legends he'd heard from "the oldest Spanish families" concerning local Native Americans who'd been killed by an invasion of Aztecs from Mexico.

> ...in the days before the face of white men had been seen along the Coast of Southern California... there occurred an Indian massacre, when all of the inhabitants of a Topango village were killed by a marauding enemy that fell upon them. The bodies of the dead were piled in a heap, according to the prevailing custom, covered with stones, and a funeral pyre burned over their heads. The fire thus started, so the legend runs, leaped deep into the fissures between the rocks; it gave birth to the mountain, whose intermittent smoking continues to this day.
>
> —"Will They Be Interpreted?" *Los Angeles Times*, 1911-02-05

The Burning Mountain was a real phenomenon that existed by today's Bel-Air Bay Club. Oil deposits are suspected as the cause of an underground fire that burned there for hundreds of years, until 1944.

Coolbaugh was especially captivated by a polished bone statuette on which "The eyes and nose of the hand made god show plainly." He said it was a royal scepter, comparing it to one that explorer Francis Drake had observed in 1579.

Anthropologist Alfred Kroeber describes a wand used by local tribes in his *Handbook of the Indians of California* (1925).

> The Jimson-weed cult is intimately associated with beliefs in a deity called… Chungichnish…. The *paviut* was a hand wand a foot and a half long, associated with the Chungichnish cult. It consisted of a board more or less pointed below, somewhat flaring at the upper end, where it was inlaid with haliotis, and tipped with a crystal or large flint.

The attention Coolbaugh received must have made him more of a nuisance to authorities because, in March 1911, a deputy sheriff forced him off his homestead. As questionable as his stewardship of the Native American mound may have been, without him all studies ceased.

In May 1911, a cast of hundreds trampled the area while making a Western called *Crossing the American Prairies in the Early Fifties*. Never released, the film was about Native Americans attacking a wagon train, and "Of course virtue in the form of the frontiersmen triumphed." It was directed by D. W. Griffith (1875-1948), whose most famous film *The Birth of a Nation* (1915) praised the Ku Klux Klan.

In September 1911, a Western was made at the mound itself. The film, called *A Chance Shot*, was directed by Pat Hartigan (1881-1951) and starred Ruth Roland (1892-1937). Its publicity irreverently boasted that it had used the artifacts as props. The fate of this film is unknown. The racist plot was summarized as…

> Red Fox, an Indian brave, wins White Doe, the chief's daughter, but to emphasize the fickleness of the Indian husband he be-

> comes enamored of Mary, a settler's daughter. Finding that his pleas for her love have no effect on the white girl he captures her and [binds] her to a tree....
>
> —IMDb, www.imdb.com/title/tt0195591

In June 1911, the *Los Angeles Herald* published a story about a Spanish priest at the San Gabriel Mission, Eugene Surgranes, who'd built a museum of artifacts, many of which he'd dug up himself. "The Topango region proved a very fertile ground."

Jesus Santa Maria (1849-1944), Topanga's first settler, had another impressive collection.

> ...this collection increased through the years to become his stock in trade many years later.... Proudly he would show his strange collection of Indian curios, odd rock formations and local fossils. There was such a demand for the articles that Jesus decided to build a small lath house in which to display them and open a curio shop.
>
> —*A History of Topanga* by Ivan L. Nelson, serialized in *Topanga Journal*, 1952-01-18

Russell K. Hart (1898-1967), Santa Monica mayor during the 1950s, said that he had collected artifacts from the mound as a boy.

Where these three collections are today is unknown, although Santa Maria did donate a portion to the Los Angeles Museum.

In October 1911, dozens of graves with artifacts were discovered at Malibu Canyon beach. Similarities between the sites led to speculation that the Natives of Topanga Beach had made these burials too.

In January 1912, University of California anthropologist Nels C. Nelson (1875-1964) recorded the Topanga mound in his "Archaeological Reconnaissance Notes" on coastal sites in Southern California.

> At the time of the examination the mound proper promiscuously dug over measured approximately 50 feet in diameter and about 6 feet in height, but the refuse scatters over an area of about 100 x 300 feet.
>
> The composition contains a great deal of earth and beach rocks but many mussel, clam and abalone shells are present. Human and animal bones were observed and many fragments of well worked mortars and pestles were found.

A few of the fragments Nelson found are still at the University of California Berkeley in the Phoebe A. Hearst Museum of Anthropology.

In September 1914, a new discovery was made by ground squirrels, whose burrows were observed to contain dark earth, human bones, and shells. The underground source of these artifacts, in the vicinity of the mound, could not be determined.

In 1915, deputy sheriffs stopped allowing people onto the old homestead property. Anxious to find out what had become of the artifacts, Professor Buell got permission to explore the area in August. He reported that "a carload of Indian relics are lying on the surface," and complained that he wasn't allowed to do further research.

In July 1916, Deputy Sheriff Edward M. Williams amused himself by exhuming artifacts (including a tomahawk) that he sent to the Los Angeles Museum. Where they are now is unknown.

Also in 1916, a Tongva Native named Setimo Lopez told ethnologist John P. Harrington that the word "Topanga" came from the Chumash Ventureño language, which implied that the Chumash boundary was farther south than had previously been thought. José Maria Zalvidea, another Tongva Native, told Harrington that there had been a cemetery at Topanga Beach with whale bones as markers, and that many of his ancestors were buried there.

In January 1923, the *Los Angeles Times* lamented that history was being destroyed by the new coast highway that was being paved across the mound (instead of curving around it like before).

In the 1930s, the Radiant Springs Water company was bottling the water from a popular roadside spring two miles up the Canyon. According to owner Joy R. Pierce (1891-1961), who lived with his family by the lagoon, "the spring was known to the Indians, who came from as far south as San Diego to get water from it to give to the sick."

In the 1940s or '50s, the mound was given the Native American site number LAN-133 by Sophie Bayler, who wrote that it had contained beads, abalone spangles, and flint arrowheads.

In 1950, another Native site, LAN-215, was recorded on nearby Parker Mesa (later Sunset Mesa) by archaeologist S. L. Peck, who noted that most of it had already been destroyed by plowing.

In 1961, the Parker Mesa site was rediscovered by anthropologist Dr. Chester King and archaeologist Tom Blackburn. Artifacts found there included bowl fragments, a basalt projectile point, a chert knife, sharpened animal bones, a partial house floor, a circular pit thought to be a yucca-roasting oven, and stones that were shaped into discs, mortar blanks, balls, and crescents. The site was estimated to have been inhabited until at least 1000 B.C., making it much older than the one at Topanga Beach. Unfortunately, the scientists had little time to study it before grading for the Sunset Mesa housing development began.

In the 1960s and '70s, Topanga Beach residents found several artifacts like rock bowls, arrowheads, beads, grinding stones, and a carved rock that appeared to have been hung on a string. Nevertheless, when State Parks took over the beach in the late '70s, archaeologist P. Barclay wrote that he'd found no evidence of the site and declared it completely destroyed.

In the 1980s, State Parks reported finding shell midden. In 2001, when they bought the rest of Lower Topanga, they made a new survey of the land. "Eight previously unrecorded sites were discovered, containing a variety of artifacts," according to *The Topanga Story* edited by Louise York and Michele Johnson (2012).

In 2002-3, State Parks archaeological monitor Sarah Jenkins drilled several feet underground and pulled up shell fragments and artifacts.

In 2004, Topanga Ranch Motel resident and Tongva tribal litigator John Tommy Rosas nominated the Lower Topanga area as a Native American Sacred Site, while fighting his and the community's eviction.

In 2007, as some of the last houses were being bulldozed, further State Parks monitoring revealed shell midden and artifacts. Because the earth had been moved around, the discovery couldn't be attributed to LAN-133 with certainty, so it was given the separate site number LAN-3759.

Today, Topanga is known as a mountain town, but archaeologists believe that the Canyon is actually named after the Native American village that was at the beach.

Geologically, Topanga's place in the mountains is also relatively recent. This is why traces of marine life can be found throughout the hills, like the 1,800-lb. fossilized sea lion discovered by Geologist W. R. B. Osterholt (1895-1958) near Mulholland Drive.

> All media, when carefully examined, give strength to the belief that the Topanga area is of marine origin and that none of its structure is continental, as for instance, the palisades upon which the city of Santa Monica are located.
>
> —*A History of Topanga* by Ivan L. Nelson, serialized in *Topanga Journal*, 1951-06-01

Only six Topanga Beach Native Americans are recorded in mission records. They are Luis Juan Athacge, 17 (baptized on August 19, 1793), Juan Antonio, 50 (baptized in 1800), and four children (baptized on March 6, 1803).

CHAPTER 2

W. W. Coolbaugh and Jack Rabbit Lodge

Colonel William Wills Coolbaugh (1839-1912) was 70 years old in 1909 when he bought the only cabin at Topanga Beach from a fisherman named Harry Johnson.

For years, this hermit house had been used exclusively by fishermen, and Johnson was the last of that finny fraternity who could call the beach his own. According to a Santa Monica Hotel register, "Harry Johnson and nurse" may have come from Evansville, IN in 1876 when he was still a baby. In adulthood, Johnson fathered two children that died in infancy, the last in 1902, which is the same year that he moved to Topanga Beach. No other details about his life could be found.

W. W. Coolbaugh (as he preferred to be called), was an optimist who jumped at new opportunities. He had moved to Topanga Beach because he believed that the seven-acre property surrounding his cabin was "formed by tidal action" and therefore had never been surveyed by the government. He intended to claim this land as a homesteader and began to cultivate it, naming his cabin Jack Rabbit Lodge.

Life at the beach suited him, and his presence there soon seemed like a natural part of the landscape.

The old delta philosopher… finds "books in the running brook /

> Sermons in stone, and good in everything...." Here he is monarch of all he surveys. He enjoys all the rights of a squatter, and is patiently awaiting the coming of the government surveyors and the day for making his final proof.
>
> —"Will They Be Interpreted?" *Los Angeles Times*, 1911-02-05

The year 1906 had seen the collapse of Arch Rock—a picturesque impediment that once stood where Mastro's Ocean Club is today—allowing better roads and cars to access Topanga Beach. Since Malibu was private and Topanga was primitive, Jack Rabbit Lodge became the popular stopping place, relieving Coolbaugh's isolation with frequent visitors. "There he entertained his friends and served coffee or lunch from his private stores to weary or belated travelers."

In 1910, Coolbaugh's tall tales about the Native American burial mound discovered on his property brought more attention to Topanga Beach. His own past was similarly shaped by flights of fancy.

Born on October 19, 1839, in Stroudsburg, PA, Coolbaugh was widely known for having been a Civil War colonel and "for having superintended the construction of several important buildings and stretches of railway in the east and south"—in particular, the Chicago Alley Elevated Railroad, or The "L," which opened in 1892.

In 1866, he married Anna (1848-1913), and they had four children. They headed west around 1900, moving to Colorado, New Mexico, and finally California.

In 1904, they bought a 1.5-acre tract in the Strawberry Park neighborhood of Gardena. In 1905, they began selling off portions of their property, likely because of a divorce. In 1906, Coolbaugh appeared to be living alone in the Ocean Park neighborhood of Santa Monica.

Coolbaugh was interested in inventions. In 1893, he was awarded for his design of a bathtub seat by the Chicago Department of Plumbing and Sanitary Materials. In 1905, he submitted a machine for incinerating garbage to Los Angeles City Hall.

He was also interested in mining. In 1906, following a tip from a dying man, he went in search of a lost gold mine in the Santa Monica Mountains. (Gold mines were reported in Tuna Canyon in 1895, so his plan didn't seem that far-fetched.) When he returned weeks later, announcing that he'd actually found the mine, newspapers began to speculate about a second California Gold Rush. However, the gold never appeared, and Coolbaugh was soon back in the mountains chasing new leads.

This pattern of big announcements without results kept repeating. In an attempt to lure investors, he banded together with other miners to form the Ocean Park Prospecting and Developing Company in 1908, telling the press…

> …sufficient minerals can be found to keep 1,000 men employed for years to come, and when the area is thoroughly developed it will surprise the country….
>
> It is my prediction that within the next ten years the Santa Monica range will resound with the noise of oil derricks and mining machinery of almost every kind. The canyons will be thickly inhabited and the at present primitive roadways will have been improved until almost every nook and corner of that inaccessible country will be opened up….
>
> —"Santa Monica Range Abounds in Wealth"
> *Los Angeles Herald*, 1908-06-19

Fortunately for the beautiful Santa Monica Mountains, Coolbaugh again couldn't back up his claims. Yet no matter how many times he failed (sometimes risking his life, like when he barely outran a brush fire in Las Flores Canyon), he always believed that success was just within reach.

The discovery of the Native American burial mound must have been deeply satisfying for him after years of trying to impress people with important finds. Although not what he'd been searching for, the mound was still a kind of treasure, and he immediately saw the opportunity in it. He sold some of the artifacts, left others on display for visitors, and enjoyed building himself up as a local celebrity—while also surely thinking that the attention would help establish his homestead. However, it had the opposite effect. The city was expanding rapidly, Topanga Beach didn't seem so distant anymore, and Coolbaugh's claim on the land was aggressive compared to when it had just been a wild place used by fishermen.

Neighboring landowners began to contest his right to live there, and on March 22, 1911, the Los Angeles Title Insurance and Trust Company, who'd claimed the land since about 1899, sent attorney Mell Frasier and a deputy sheriff to evict Coolbaugh. The two men piled his belongings in the road, then set Jack Rabbit Lodge on fire, burning down two outbuildings in the process.

The questionable legality of this eviction appeared even more so when Coolbaugh revealed that he had recently sold Jack Rabbit Lodge to a Santa Monica company with plans to turn it into a private clubhouse. He threatened to sue but never went to court, perhaps because the new owner was his own Ocean Park Company.

Dispirited, Coolbaugh returned to Ocean Park, floating between hotels and private residences. There were also hospital stays as his health began to mysteriously decline. His last residence was in Echo Park, where he died at age 73 on March 21, 1912. The fact that he died one day before the anniversary of his Topanga Beach eviction and his poor mental state seem to indicate a suicide.

> After his eviction he seemed to lose interest in things of [this] earth and his death was a natural dissolution rather than the result of [a] mortal disease.
>
> —"Eccentric Character," *Los Angeles Times*, 1912-03-22

Coolbaugh's one-paragraph obituary, ungraciously titled "Eccentric Character," said only of his past that he was a Civil War veteran and a pioneer of Southern California. It didn't mention that he had built the Chicago Alley Elevated Railroad. The only evidence I could find that he did is the hearsay printed in California newspapers, and a census record showing that he had once been a "Railroad Agent."

A Civil War website confirms that Coolbaugh was wounded at the Battle of Chancellorsville in Virginia while fighting for the North on May 3, 1863, but it also says that he was promoted from a private to a commissary-sergeant. If he ever became a colonel, it would have had to be through military service after the war.

Further research shows that there was a Colonel Coolbaugh in the Civil War who was Superintendent of Military Railroads, a known conman who was always looking for investors and claiming to have access to gold mines. His name was George Coolbaugh (b.1834), and he was the brother of prominent Chicago banker William Findlay Coolbaugh (1821-1877). What became of him later in life is uncertain.

George was born one county away from W. W. Coolbaugh, but I haven't been able to establish a connection between them. For now, their commonalities are just a curious coincidence.

CHAPTER 3

Rancho Boca de Santa Monica

In 1827, about 25 years after the last Native Americans departed Topanga Beach, the land was given to Antonio Ignacio Machado and Francisco Javier Alvarado by Mexico as part of a 6,656-acre grant called the Rancho Boca de Santa Monica.

The next owners, Ysidro Reyes (1813-1861) and Francisco Marquez (1798-1850), were the first settlers to actually live on the Rancho, building permanent structures at the eponymous "mouth" of Santa Monica Canyon in 1838. They maintained their claim after California changed hands in the Mexican-American War in 1848.

When the land was divided among their children, Marquez's son Bonifacio (1838-1891) was given Topanga Beach. Much of the rest of the Rancho was sold off in the early 1870s to Colonel Robert S. Baker (1826-1894) and Nevada Senator John P. Jones (1829-1912), co-founders of the city of Santa Monica.

> Those were the days before the cities of the Southwest learned that co-operation and not competition is the surest way to the success of all, and certain groups in several of the inland communities with an eye to holding the tourist trade were lavish with disparaging tales of the winter climate of Santa Monica....
>
> [Henry J. Engelbrecht, Superintendent of the North Beach Bath House, and Juan José Carrillo (1842-1916), Santa Monica's first mayor,] arranged to hold old Spanish sports on the beach during the worst winter months to attract people to the city....

> [T]he contest which aroused the greatest interest was that called corrida del gallo ["Pull the Rooster"]. A live chicken was buried in the sand, leaving exposed only his head and neck, which was well greased to render it more difficult to grasp. The horsemen would spur past at top speed, and holding fast to the horn with the left hand, swept gracefully down from the saddle in an attempt to seize the fowl and drag him out as they sped by. Not only must the rider gauge his distance perfectly, but often as not the horse would shy at the strange wriggling object in his path, and he would come down very properly into the dust. The late Mike Marquez, a member of the well-known Marquez family of this city and regarded as one of the finest riders in the Southwest, suffered a fractured leg in such a fall on the ocean front....
>
> [By 1898,] the sport had long since been forbidden by the humane authorities, and its devotees were obliged to indulge only infrequently and out of sight and hearing of the law up the beach toward Topanga. Its last appearance in the community was... [at] a grand fiesta held by... Bonifacio... on the shore of the cove known as Las Jollitas at the mouth of [Las] Pulgas canyon....
>
> —"Santa Monica Beach Sports Once Attracted Cream of Southland's Colorful Horsemen to Compete in Most Dangerous of Tournaments" *Sunday Morning Outlook*, 1927-11-06

Bullfighting was also part of the rodeo games on the Rancho. "No Spanish community is without a bull-ring or its equivalent." There was even one in Santa Monica, "in the gulch south of Colorado street," that was later made into a bicycle race track. Today it's the 10 Freeway.

In 1899, Bonifacio's widow, Maria Antonia Olivares de Marquez, sold Lower Topanga to Edward C. Stelle (1856-1951), who in 1906 seems to have lost the property because of delinquent taxes.

CHAPTER 4

They Tramped to Topango

In 1889, a French fisherman named Pierre Aubriere (1835-1909) was living at Topanga Beach, according to a report that his cabin was robbed. Several days later, the robber was arrested in the hills wearing Aubriere's clothes and watch. Aubriere had come to Topanga Beach via San Francisco, perhaps as early as 1883, when a *San Francisco Examiner* ad for unclaimed mail listed his name.

Aubriere's legacy may have been to interest future landlords the Los Angeles Athletic Club in Topanga Beach. In 1894, nine members of the Club's "Trampers' Annex" hiked to Topanga from the new Mile Long Pier near Santa Monica Canyon. There they met and were entertained by Aubriere, whom they described as an "old Portuguese fisherman," perhaps another side of his ethnicity. The Trampers returned for a second visit in 1895. Is it possible that some of these young men, nostalgic for their Topanga visits with Aubriere, inspired the LAAC to buy the land 30 years later?

Aubriere would have seen Frederick Rindge (1857-1905) directing the construction of the first road up the coast after Rindge bought the Malibu Ranch in 1897.

He also would have seen the LA County chain gang at work on the first Topanga road, and greeted the Topanga pioneers, who came down it in 1898. Unlike today, this road had an exit on what later became Topanga Canyon Lane, so the wagons would have ended up nearly at Aubriere's doorstep. Lucy Cheney (1868-1952) was given the honor of driving the first wagon because of her persistence in making County officials recognize the need for a road. She and her husband Columbus (1851-1937) were among the first families to settle in Topanga. To celebrate, an open-pit barbecue was prepared at the lagoon by Brigadore Valdez, who had built the first house in Topanga.

However, both of these new roads were considered treacherous, and longer routes to Los Angeles were still relied on.

In 1907, a search for bandits led police to Topanga Beach, where they encountered a "halfbreed, who spoke a polyglot mixture and confessed to a name which sounded like a printer's pi," or Latin placeholder text. This deplorable description could only refer to Aubriere.

> The detectives could not determine clearly whether it was yesterday morning or a week ago yesterday that the man had seen something, but his enthusiasm made up for the lack of small details and his testimony was encouraging.
>
> —"Follow Clews to Vanishing Point," *Los Angeles Herald*, 1907-02-14

Topanga Beach fishermen subsisted by ocean fishing. The earliest account I could find of creek fishing, from 1903, said that "some excellent catches have been reported already from the Topanga." However, the creek was restocked by the State Fish and Game Commission in 1909 and 1922, making it likely that they'd first stocked it around 1900. This is significant, considering that one reason for evicting the Lower Topanga neighborhood in 2006 was to restore the "natural habitat" of the steelhead trout.

In 1910, car salesman E. Roger Stearns made a publicity stunt out of fishing from the seat of his red Velie, and in 1913, J. Smeaton Chase (1864-1923) wrote in his book *California Coast Trails* that "The stream contained some fair-sized trout," but by 1918 the fish were gone.

> If the Topango brook ever held a trout it must have been in the

> days when the red man roamed the hills.
>
> —"Fishing for Trout a Sad Stunt in Topango"
> *Santa Monica Outlook*, 1918-05-01

In 1921, fisherman Alexander MacKenzie proved that fish could still be found by hiking deep into the Canyon. He also noted, "Water snakes abounded, every pool containing two or three."

The two-striped garter snake continues to make its home in the creek. It is a natural enemy of trout, as Topanga bus driver Raymond James observed in 1916.

> This morning as James was driving his car down the mountain boulevard he noticed a great commotion in the stream at his left. Soon he saw a trout leap out of the water and in its jaws was a large-sized water-snake. The snake had wrapped itself around the trout and was doing its best to impede its movements.
>
> —"Battle Royal Between Fish and Reptile"
> *Santa Monica Bay Outlook*, 1916-07-14

In 1902, the US Board on Geographic Names settled on the name Topanga… "Not Tobanao, Tobanca, nor Topango." Confusingly, "Topango" was still preferred for decades, and Topanga Beach was considered to be part of Santa Monica because it belonged to the old Rancho.

Before 1911, there was rarely more than one cabin at Topanga Beach, yet many sightseers were drawn to the end of the public road, and to the 30-foot Arch Rock that spanned it at the present-day site of Mastro's Ocean Club. Countless photos were taken in front of this popular proto-Instagram backdrop.

Native and Latin American histories said that Arch Rock had once been much bigger, and recalled the roar of the ocean as it rushed through at high tide.

Frederick Rindge perceived Arch Rock as the natural gateway to his Malibu Ranch, even though the actual gate was at Las Flores Canyon.

> This rock was the especial favorite of the late F. H. Rindge, who, when letting the contract for the grading of the road up the beach, inserted a special clause in the memorandum of agreement with the contractor that Arch Rock was to be neither defaced nor disturbed in any particular.
>
> —"Arch Rock Mystery," *Los Angeles Daily Times*, 1906-03-26

One plan to protect Arch Rock from a proposed railroad was to build a tunnel under what is now Sunset Mesa.

Rindge's connection to Arch Rock strangely continued in death. Both grew weaker in the winter of 1905, and both collapsed within half a year of each other. Rindge fell into a diabetic coma and never recovered. Arch Rock fell in a storm.

> The heavy rainfall of last night proved too much for picturesque Arch Rock.... Little by little it has been crumbling and melting away. The storms of last winter weakened the arch and when the road graders removed the crumbling portions it was seen that it could not endure much longer.
>
> —"Pretty Arch Rock Is No More," *The Daily Outlook*, 1906-03-24

The supporting column, on the beach side, did not break, but road workers removed it with the rest of the debris anyway. This may have contributed to rumors that "enthusiastic railway promoters" had blown up Arch Rock, even though the rise of cars soon obviated the need for a railroad. The last remnant of Arch Rock, on the cliff side, was demolished in 1915 to move the beach road away from the high tide line.

Before cars, the favorite mode of transportation to Topanga Beach was a hayride. The Arcadia Hotel in Santa Monica regularly toured guests there. Leo Carrillo (1880-1961), later a famous actor, enjoyed picnics and deer hunting there.

On June 27, 1906, over 150 Methodists held their annual picnic at Tuna Canyon. Their caravan included five large wagons draped in bunting for the young people with G. W. Schutte's Boys' Brass Band playing in the first wagon. On the way home, the girls stopped to play baseball at the mouth of Topanga.

Another noteworthy excursion happened in September 1910, when a wagon-full of chaperoned teenagers camped for a week at Topanga Beach.

> There were a couple of kodaks in the party, and some interesting pictures were taken of the interesting places around the camp and of the different members of the party.
>
> —"In Social Circles," *The Daily Outlook*, 1910-09-19

The accidental repetition of "interesting" is fitting since this was the summer of the Stanford field trip, W. W. Coolbaugh's homestead, and the Native American burial mound. If only we had those pictures!

The last large gathering of this period was on July 16, 1911, when 75 guests attended "an old-fashioned Rhode Island clam bake" for employees of Levy's Cafe, the humble name of Los Angeles's biggest restaurant. Located downtown, it could seat 1% of the city's population, and had its own house orchestra. Owner Al Levy (1860-1941) hosted the beach party, with assistance from manager B. W. Singer, cashier "Fat" Henry, and head waiters Arthur Godfrey and Will Canon. After lunch, the "Levy negro minstrels" entertained with song and dance. Levy was an enthusiastic member of the Elks, and likely attended their rodeo at Topanga Beach in 1923.

The parties came to an end when deputy sheriffs took control of the beach. Camping was prohibited, and a prison camp was built.

CHAPTER 5

The Chain Gang

The LA County Prison chain gang had been in Topanga on and off since 1898, when they worked on the first road through the Canyon.

A stockade was built near the beach in September 1911 to house them while they were doing improvement work, but two months later a brush fire passed through and likely burned it.

Another prison camp was built in April 1913, when the chain gang was tasked with building a whole new Topanga road that would stay on the south side of the creek until the S-turns, eliminating the inconvenience of multiple crossings. The camp had…

> …a large steel cage where the men are kept. This cage is covered with a tent and inside the bunks are placed tier upon tier so that there are sleeping quarters for nearly a hundred men….
>
> The "village" is the last word in neatness, and the rock bordered walks from tent to tent, with the trees and canyon as a background, make a beautiful scene.
>
> —"Santa Monica's Points of Beauty and Interest,"
> *The Daily Outlook*, 1913-07-26

The embellishments were thanks to Sheriff William Hammel (1865-1932), who had campaigned for…

> …country quarters for prisoners where open-air occupations

> can be provided in the effort to make better citizens of wrongdoers… not down on the river bottom, though, but on a hill, where there's plenty of fresh air and sunlight and a wide sweep of view; let's give 'em the best we've got.
>
> —"Treat 'Em Like Human Beings," *Los Angeles Times*, 1912-11-08

Other reforms Hammel fought for were to pay prisoners for their work, and to give them dignified uniforms.

> [We should] quit the idea of making clowns of the prisoners and make them look like civilized human beings by clothing them in decent suits of one color.
>
> —"Treat 'Em Like Human Beings," *Los Angeles Times*, 1912-11-08

Within a year, the chain gang was earning $1.50 a day, and their blue-and-black suits were changed to brown.

Clearly, Hammel was an idealistic and ethical man. He was childhood best friends with one of Los Angeles's first Hispanic sheriffs, Martin Aguirre (1858-1929). When Hammel became sheriff in 1899, he brought Aguirre back into the department as a deputy.

Hammel also hired Los Angeles's first African American deputy sheriff, Julius Loving (1863-1938). The next sheriff fired Loving, but Hammel was later reelected and rehired Loving, who rose in the ranks to become one of the most respected men in the department.

But Hammel's idealism sometimes blinded him or made him conceited. He called the prison camp the "Hammel Recreation Camp," and the new road the "Hammel Highway." When he brought the LA County Board of Supervisors to inspect the work, he treated them to a surprise barbecue. They then lectured the prisoners about dignity, patriotism, and the unfairness of their plight, and gave them a half-day off to swim in the lagoon. The day's "entertainment" continued with Hammel taking his guests to the new movie studio Inceville, where Sunset meets PCH today, to see a silent film and meet the Native American tribe that lived there as Western actors.

Others shared Hammel's disconnect about what was really going on with the chain gang, whose typical crimes were vagrancy, failure to support their families, and assault.

The Daily Outlook article titled "Points of Beauty and Interest" featured the prison camp next to the La Brea Tar Pits, and described it in the same touristy language. Of the prisoners, the article said, "They are a happy and contented lot, for they are kindly treated and well fed and the work is not very hard."

Another article conjured up a vision of the camp that could have been painted by Thomas Kinkade.

> The picture presented was one for the brush of an artist.... The great dormitory sits in the center of what will soon be a beautiful garden. The prisoners have already marked off the plot for flower designs....
>
> —"Would Abolish Convict Labor," *Los Angeles Times*, 1913-05-14

A third article listed "frequent sea baths" and "an increase in manliness" as some of the benefits of being in the Topanga chain gang, as if it were the Junior Lifeguards. The jailers, appearing to be on vacation, "pitched tents for their wives and families during the summer season" on the opposite side of the creek.

On July 29, 1914, Al F. Young (1875-1935), a Santa Monica real estate agent and Elk, started a bus line to Topanga Beach that he advertised as a sightseeing tour.

> First there is Santa Monica canyon itself, said to be the place where vast pirate treasures have been hidden. Then there is the long wharf, the longest in the world, and just beyond this is the Japanese village, always a source of wonder to visitors in California. The burning mountain, whose fame is nation-wide and

> whose solution is the enigma of scientists is seen on this trip. Santa Ynez canyon and the famous moving picture camp and village is one of the main stops.... The county convict camp at the mouth of the [Topanga] canyon always proves a point of interest and is within a stone's throw of the terminus of the line.
>
> —"Bus Line on Coast," *The Daily Outlook*, 1914-07-28

Santa Monica Librarian Elfie Mosse (1868-1939) started a feel-good campaign to bring the prisoners donated books, although she cautioned that "Too sensational literature is not desired."

But the unhappiness of the chain gang couldn't be denied.

In February 1914, Margarita Castor walked from Oxnard to Los Angeles to beg for the release of her husband Cacino, who had stolen a suitcase. Her devotion persuaded a judge to release Cacino on probation, and moved Deputy Sheriff Martin Aguirre to "pass the hat" in the department for Cacino.

There were also many prison breaks. The biggest was on August 26, 1915, when 10 men, relying on a noisy generator to mask the sound of filing through the bars, escaped through the roof of their cage and fled into the hills.

The escapee who caused the most alarm was Native American Francisco Flores, a repeat criminal who had already served time for an 1895 attempted murder. "Flores, Firewater, Fight" was the *Los Angeles Herald* headline describing that shooting, which seriously wounded another member of his tribe.

Flores was from the Zanja de Cota reservation in Santa Barbara County. In 1896, he went to court to protest a church group that was trying to steal his tribe's land.

By 1899, he was routinely getting locked up in Los Angeles for small thefts and vagrancy. "He costs the city too much for gasoline.... We have to haul him to the station in a patrol wagon too much," a police officer quipped.

The *Los Angeles Times*, describing Flores's beaten demeanor in court, said, "He listened to the sentence and warning with stoical indifference, not seeming to care whether he was in jail or at liberty."

Flores successfully vanished after the prison break.

J. B. Hernan was imprisoned for not supporting his wife. He got out of his chains with the help of fellow inmates and escaped by jumping off a Topanga cliff in 1917. However, when he tried to reconcile with his wife, she refused and turned him back in.

Charlie Chaplin (1889-1977) parodied an escape from the Topanga Beach prison camp in *The Adventurer* (1917), where he can be seen running from deputy sheriffs at the entrance to the Canyon.

The new Topanga road was completed on May 29, 1915, and for the first time it went straight through to the Valley. A celebration was held by the Automobile Club of Southern California, this time at the Top of Topanga. Afterwards, a parade of cars, decorated with pennants, drove down and back to the city. No stop was made at the beach.

The chain gang immediately began working on new projects, like building the road up Tuna Canyon and raising the coast road. By the end of their time at Topanga Beach, about 1917, their enchanting myth had disintegrated like the American flag flying over their prison.

> The miserable apology for the nation's emblem is weather-worn, tattered and faded, and flutters in pathetic ribbons before the gaze of hundreds of auto parties bound over the coast road or through the scenic canyon.
>
> —"Flag in Distress," *Santa Monica Bay Outlook*, 1916-07-10

Chain gangs were abolished in 1921, but like an echo of their distress, a weathered flag still flies over Topanga Beach.

CHAPTER 6

Silents at the Beach

During the same years that the chain gang had its permanent camp at Topanga Beach, 1913-1916, the silent movie studio Inceville was operating one mile away, where Sunset Blvd. is today. Its founder was Thomas Ince (1880-1924), the "Father of the Western," and he ensured the integrity of his films by not only employing 300 cowboys, but a whole Sioux tribe (200 men, women, and children who lived on the grounds in tepees). One of his most successful films was *Custer's Last Fight* (1912), which showed the side of the Native Americans, and featured some who had actually been in the battle. The Topanga Beach party atmosphere of earlier days now shifted here, as people came to see the movie stars and spectacle—especially in May, when Inceville's annual Wild West Rodeo and Barbecue drew thousands.

Before the prison camp imposed its restrictions, Topanga Beach had also been the setting for early movies. The most notable one was *Crossing the American Prairies in the Early Fifties* by D. W. Griffith (1875-1948), a single-reel film, about 15 minutes long, produced by the American Biograph Company in May 1911. In the film, Native Americans attack a wagon train at night, capturing some of the pioneers and slaughtering the rest. The survivors escape burning at the stake and other terrors before finally reaching California, while the dead are buried by the shifting sands. Unlike Ince's films, Griffith's film assumed the Native Americans to be evil. Four years later, Griffith would reignite the Ku Klux

Klan with his film *The Clansman* (renamed *The Birth of a Nation*).

Griffith directed *Crossing the American Prairies in the Early Fifties* through a megaphone from the saddle of a cream-colored horse. He included 200 cowboys from nearby ranches, 50 women and children, 120 horses, and 11 prairie schooners. A reporter observed…

> On approach the camp of the players resembles that of a large circus. There are two big tents of perhaps 500 capacity, and about twenty smaller tents. There is a commissary department, which rivals a downtown hotel in its completeness, for it must be remembered that these moving picture folks are high-priced artists, and accustomed from years of travel to the best that the land affords.
>
> —"Making the World's Greatest Film Here"
> *Los Angeles Times*, 1911-05-15

The most difficult part of the filming was saved for last, when the partially buried actors had to play dead as dirt blew into their eyes, mouth, ears, and hair. "There were heard smothered oaths from the dead people that no wild cowboy had ever excelled," remembered Griffith's wife Linda Arvidson (1884-1949). Many of the actors threatened to quit, even though it was the last day. The women were particularly unhappy because they had to wear grungy men's clothes to make the battlefield appear larger. Their dreams of appearing on film were dashed by the fear of being recognized in such an unflattering role.

A young woman named Myrtle Dennison of Caney, KS was cast in a leading role, prompting her local newspaper to gush that she had "attained quite an achievement in the world of art." Veteran actors Dell Henderson (1883-1956) and W. Chrystie Miller (1843-1922) were also in the film.

After the final scene, everyone rushed home for a thorough scrubbing and shampoo. Then came the bad news: there was static in the film. Griffith demanded a reshoot, and ordered the actors back to their places in the dirt. Sadly, this extra effort was wasted because the film is listed online as unreleased… even though I found one theater in Salt Lake City, UT that advertised it in July 1911.

CHAPTER 7

Elkhorn Camp

Revelry returned to Lower Topanga after the roadwork was completed, the chain gang began to move away, and the first of many fires began to destroy Inceville.

A resort named Elkhorn Camp was built along the creek, a mile and a half from the beach. It had seven cabins, a cafe, an open-air dance hall, and a shooting gallery. The creek was dammed to create a lake, and a small goldfish pond was "one of the major attractions."

I can't find any mention of Elkhorn Camp until 1921, but *The Topanga Story* says that it was rebuilt after being destroyed in a 1916 flood. It couldn't have existed earlier than 1915, when the new Topanga road was completed.

According to *Southern California's Prettiest Drive* by Francis Brunner (1925), the proprietor was W. L. Woods, and the manager was M. A. Callanan. A man named Walter L. Woods was a member of the local Elks, and I wonder if Elkhorn Camp was created by that fraternity, which was active in Lower Topanga in the 1920s.

Elkhorn Camp was managed in the early 1930s by Francis J. Perry, and known as Perry's Camp. In 1935, new owner Lillian Fields (1883-1941) renamed it Woodland Gardens, then Woodland Springs.

The resort burned down in the November 1938 fire.

CHAPTER 8

Police Parties

Deputy Sheriff Edward M. Williams (1876-1940) is the next person known to have lived on Topanga Beach, five years after W. W. Coolbaugh's house was burned down there… possibly by Williams himself!

The Title Insurance and Trust Company assigned Williams to guard their property, but he also helped chase down escapees in the hills during the last months of the prison camp. One escapee who eluded him was Vera Gonzales, a young man who had failed to support his wife and children. Gonzales's escape was so flawless that no one could understand how he broke out of the cage.

Despite his policing, Williams began a trend of relaxing restrictions at Topanga Beach. Formerly a St. Louis billiard-hall owner, he was a social man and a member of the Elks. He kicked off the summer of 1916 with a barbecue that was celebrated "into the wee sma' hours of the night" beside huge pits near the lagoon. On the guest list were…

> Sheriff [John] Cline with a small army of vigilant deputies… jurists, politicians, court attaches, actors, writers….
>
> After the closing hour of cabaret cafes in the beach cities and Los Angeles the performers [joined] the al fresco throng.
>
> —"Free Comrades Will Gather at Barbecue"
> *Santa Monica Bay Outlook*, 1916-06-05

At the end of the summer, Williams hosted a venison barbecue. This was an annual tradition started by Columbus Cheney (1851-1937) to celebrate the opening of deer season in Topanga. George Cheney (1895-1975), his 21-year-old son, decided to move the barbecue to Williams's place to make it more accessible to guests coming from Santa Monica and Malibu.

Along with the relaxing of restrictions came more opportunities for abuse and crime.

Just like his predecessor, Williams diverted himself by digging up Native American artifacts. Skeletons, tomahawks, and pottery were some of the discoveries he made. Another discovery was a rusty harpoon embedded in a beached swordfish that bore the words "Lee" and "1861." The significance of the old harpoon is unclear since swordfish only live about 10 years. Symbolically, it seems more significant that the dead swordfish appeared shortly after the Chumash graves had been dug up again. The Chumash believed that all creatures in the ocean have their counterparts on land: lobsters were potato bugs, sardines were lizards, and swordfish were humans.

In February 1917, Police Officer T. J. P. Shannon reported a large smugglers' boat using a red lantern to communicate with a car at Topanga Beach. Both the boat and car vanished before they could be investigated, but authorities were "confident that the ship landed no Chinese or opium or other smuggled goods." Chinese immigrants were smuggled in for cheap labor during this time.

In April 1918, a robbery was committed at the Last Chance store and home of the Hall family on the coast road near the mouth of Topanga. William Hall returned to find his store broken into after dropping off his children at school in Santa Monica. Missing were two gold necklaces, two diamond rings, and a turquoise ring. The store was also looted of simpler luxuries like fruit, candy, and chewing gum, leading Hall to suspect that the culprits were children.

Whoever the robbers were, Hall himself may have been a

shadier character. In 1912, a Newport Beach bartender named William Hall fired a dozen times with a shotgun to stop three bank robbers from escaping. They still got away, but a fisherman was hit and had to be saved by surgery. In 1916, a Santa Monica bartender named William Hall was working at the Gilman Saloon on 2nd Street when it was raided for gambling. Hall claimed ignorance, but police saw him run to the back to stop a craps game when they entered.

In April 1917, the US joined World War I, sparking outbursts of patriotism. During the first week, more than 100 men joined the Santa Monica Home Guard, including Deputy Sheriff Williams, who enlisted as a mounted scout and offered to bring his own horse. Williams also made his Topanga Beach home a headquarters to register for the draft.

A memorable wartime party was thrown in May 1918 by a young couple named Walter B. Dorrer and Ruth Larson. Japanese lanterns were strung along the beach, carpets were spread on the sand, and 40 guests danced to the music of a record player. Suddenly the couple changed into wedding clothes and a surprise ceremony began. The guests were shocked because the couple hadn't even announced their engagement. The press dubbed this a "camouflage wedding." It wasn't a legal wedding because Dorrer had to leave for the army immediately, but the couple still wanted to exchange vows. Their pretend preacher extracted a "promise of no camouflage affairs for either young person" while they were apart.

CHAPTER 9

Cooper's Camp

In the summer of 1918, the growing number of campers on the beach in Santa Monica was making the locals anxious.

> ...the tents have no sanitary arrangements and... some of the campers are not careful about the attire they wear on the sand.
>
> —"Other Side Will Confer with Mayor"
> *Santa Monica Outlook*, 1918-07-30

The city decided that a campsite was needed, so in 1919, Camp Topango was built on an outlying beach to hide these low-income tourists. It was managed by Miller Cooper (1869-1944), and later became known as Cooper's Camp, which helped differentiate it from an earlier Camp Topanga that had existed in Old Topanga Canyon between 1909-1916.

Miller lived at the beach with his family, including his brother, Deputy Sheriff Archie Cooper (1883-1932), who guarded the property for the Title Insurance and Trust Company.

Camp Topango was immediately popular, but also immediately drew bad press. One of its attractions was a dance pavilion with live music by "the famous Moon Light Four." In 1919, an employee named Hazel Pritchard gave an account to police of a suspicious man who showed up there.

> On the night of July 4 we had quite a crowd dancing. I was at

> the gate in charge when a man came down the road on foot. An admission of 25 cents is charged to persons in cars and I asked him where his automobile was. "I left it up the road," he said. I told him I thought he could go in free. After leaving the gate I danced with him and he introduced himself as Mr. New. He was a very poor dancer and acted strangely. Some of the people at the camp had heard a shot up the road before this. He was there less than an hour and went back up the road.
>
> —"Canyon 'Dance of Death' Denied by Love Tragedy Man"
> *Los Angeles Evening Herald*, 1919-07-12

The man was Harry S. New Jr. (1887-1950), who later that night turned himself into police with the body of his girlfriend Freda Lesser (1899-1919) in his car. New had shot Lesser on a drive to Topanga after she told him that she was pregnant but wouldn't marry him or keep the child.

Hazel's "Dance of Death" story was corroborated by Miller, who said he'd seen New many times at camp dances. Then things started to unravel. Pritchard was revealed to also be working for New's attorney, John L. Richardson, who pretended astonishment at her tale, while probably having invented it himself to help New's insanity plea. Both Pritchard and Miller later said that they were misquoted, and that New had not danced at Camp Topango the night he shot Lesser.

In 1920, beach cabins were built, leading to a dispute between the Cooper brothers and their landlord over who should collect the rents. In one cabin lived "Greek George" Conios (1872-1920), who moored his boat in the kelp beds. While disembarking near Santa Monica Canyon at the Mile Long Pier, which would be torn down later that year, Conios fell into high surf and disappeared. His body was "carried back almost to the door of his beach cottage," where it was found 11 days later.

The worst publicity for Camp Topango came when the Cooper brothers attacked an African American man named Arthur Valentine (1892-1967) on Memorial Day.

Valentine was born in Des Moines, IA, and lived in downtown LA off Central Ave. According to his granddaughter Jataun Valentine (b.1937), who lives in Venice today, he worked as the chauffeur for a Topanga family.

On May 30, 1920 (Memorial Day was always celebrated on May 30 then), Valentine, his wife Charlotte (1893-1958), children Arthur Jr. (1913-1969) and Gwendolyn (1914-2004), and friend Horace Walker tried to go swimming at Topanga Beach but were immediately hassled. Five-year-old Gwendolyn was pushed aside, which may have been the breaking point.

The Cooper brothers claimed that Valentine had refused to pay the fee to use their property, and that he'd defended his right to be below the mean tide line by pulling a gun. Archie disarmed him, fought him one-on-one while the others were held at gunpoint, and arrested him.

Valentine claimed that the fight was racially motivated, and that they had pistol-whipped him. Years later, the African American newspaper *The California Eagle* wrote that he'd been shot in the leg. Jataun remembers that he did have a bad leg, and that he wore a monocle to correct an injured eye. She'd heard his injuries were the result of a fight, but he never talked about his problems. Instead, she thinks he dealt with misfortune by striving harder for success. He went on to grow a side business making Black cosmetics, and then became a real estate agent.

The Cooper brothers were born in a small town called Danby, near Ithaca, NY.

Miller Cooper, the older brother, was usually mild-mannered enough to stay out of the news. Besides managing Camp Topango, he developed the land behind it into the Topango Ranch. He lived there with his wife Mary M. (b.1876), daughters Edna (1900-1989), Sarah (1907-1926), and Mary Laurania (1916-1966), mother Sarah L. Cooper (1847-1923), and father-in-law Henry Monroe (b.1841), who ran the Topango Store.

Archie Cooper was hot-headed, reckless, and stubborn. Before moving to Topanga Beach, he'd been a motorcycle cop in South Pasadena. A three-year report showed that, since he'd been hired, there were fewer warnings given, and double the number of fines and arrests. He'd been in at least six speeding accidents, miraculously escaping each time with minor injuries. Once, while pursuing a suspect, he hit a car, flew through the windshield into the passenger seat, and ordered the driver to keep up the chase. Another time, he hit a curb and flew headfirst onto the ground, lying unconscious for 10 minutes. "Only a remarkable physique saved Cooper," a doctor said.

Archie's dangerous behavior had been evident in his youth. In 1903, a streetcar returning to Los Angeles from San Pedro was held up by three masked men. The driver was beaten, and all aboard were robbed except 20-year-old Archie, who defiantly hid his money. When the robbers began cursing at the women, Archie called them cowards and challenged them to an honest fight. They threatened to shoot him if he didn't shut up. He replied that he "would make a sieve" out of them if he had a gun. Despite this provocation, the robbers only fired a few warning shots and fled.

Archie's belligerence may even have affected his childhood… if he attended Formwalt Street School in Atlanta, GA. There, in 1897, a schoolboy with his name and age teased a new classmate named Sol Williams for wearing a collar, saying, "Dogs wear collars." After school, the boys fought, and Archie stabbed Williams in the back, nearly killing him. The principal, Mrs. Gregory, acknowledged that Archie was a troublemaker. The Cooper family relocated to California around this time.

A second deputy sheriff, Canadian Frank DeWar (1883-1932), also got involved in the beach fight, either because he was living there too or just happened to be visiting for the holiday.

DeWar owed his life to Archie. In 1916, he was making a rescue in the flooded Los Angeles River when his leg and two ribs were broken by floating debris. Archie was assisting, and managed to pull him into a boat before he was swept away.

A Spanish-American War veteran, DeWar quickly bounced back. That same year, he enlisted in World War I (before the US draft!), fighting with a kilted Scottish battalion nicknamed "The Ladies from Hell." He was discharged after being gassed and having his leg scarred by shrapnel, but enlisted again to operate a tank when the US finally joined the war. His dedication earned him a letter of congratulations from former president Theodore Roosevelt (1858-1919), even though the war ended before DeWar could return to Europe.

At the time of the beach fight, DeWar was still in and out of the hospital, recovering from his injuries. It's no wonder that this tough guy went on to become Los Angeles's ultimate noir cop. He was in charge of the city's anti-gangster squad, and worked on several high-profile cases, like the trial of "The Tiger Woman" Clara Phillips (b.1899).

Miller's father-in-law Henry Monroe was also present at the beach fight and held a gun, but his participation was considered to be insignificant.

Were these men racists? It seems so. In court, their attorney Samuel S. Hahn (1888-1957) tried to justify their actions by saying that "he would not care to be close to any colored person" either. More race-baiting comments were made by their second attorney, John L. Richardson, the same man who had defended New. Richardson's involvement in their defense further suggests that Miller helped fabricate the "Dance of Death" story for New's insanity plea.

During this time, Los Angeles was experiencing a Ku Klux Klan resurgence.

In Topanga, a resort called Kneen's Kamp advertised with the initials KKK by inserting the word "Komfort" into its name (although no other connection to the Klan has been found).

In Santa Monica Canyon, "the greatest Ku Klux Klan initiation ever held in the West" took place on March 29, 1922. Cars lined the beach for more than a mile, as 300 Klansmen inducted

800 new members, with 200 others in attendance.

Weeks later, an incident called "The Inglewood Raid" led to the outing of many Klansmen who were Los Angeles officials, including Sheriff William Traeger (1880-1935), the boss of Archie and DeWar.

It's worth noting that DeWar was once accused of being in the KKK himself by an African American robbery suspect, who complained at his trial that DeWar was making faces at him. Traeger was especially close to DeWar, promoting him to Undersheriff, honoring him with a diamond-studded badge, and treating him as his successor. However, just as Traeger was about to leave office, DeWar died in a plane crash.

Police Chief Louis Oaks (1883-1938) was also outed as a Klansman. Responding to accusations that the KKK was undermining the morale of the police force, his department outrageously stated that, while 50% of its officers were indeed KKK members, it saw "no reason why the policemen cannot join the organization if they so wish, provided they perform their duties."

The Valentine case ended, after nearly three years of strategic delays in Los Angeles Superior Court, when charges against the Cooper brothers and DeWar were dismissed because of "insufficient evidence." *The California Eagle* published its assessment of what the case had meant to the African American community 25 years later.

> …while a satisfactory victory was not won, at least Negroes of this community served notice on that element seeking to establish a Jim-Crow policy on the ocean beaches, that they would fight to the last ditch to protect and preserve their citizenship rights.
>
> —"On the Sidewalk," *The California Eagle*, 1947-01-02

The embarrassment of these events led to a decrease in the KKK and its eventual outlawing in California.

African Americans decided that they needed their own beach, and began to establish their presence at Bay Street Beach in Santa Monica, where they had historically felt safe because it was near a Black church.

Bay Street Beach became an important gathering place for decades, and it's also known for producing the first recorded California surfer of color, Nick Gabaldon (1927-1951). It was added to the National Register of Historic Places in 2019.

CHAPTER 10

Helen Gibson and The Rodeo Grounds

The development of Topanga Beach happened quickly after Miller Cooper opened his campsite in 1919.

Musicians were the first group to see the potential of the new resort. In September 1920, members of the Los Angeles Symphony and the Los Angeles Philharmonic Society arranged to build cabins on the Salt Grass Lawn, as the flat land by the lagoon was called. They were George Leslie Smith, Caroline Estes Smith, William Edson Strobridge, Sylvan Noack, Mildred Marsh, Olga Steeb, and R. D. MacLean.

Olga Steeb (1890-1941) had one of her most famous performances half a year later, on March 19, 1921, when the Los Angeles Philharmonic called her from the audience to substitute for an injured soloist. Without rehearsing, she flawlessly played Camille Saint-Saëns's Piano Concerto in G Minor. She was not only a gifted musician, but a great teacher with students who also became virtuosos like composer Harry Partch (1901-1974).

The cabins were first used for weekend parties, then for a summer camp, and still stand today as the abandoned Topanga Ranch Motel.

Abraham Franklin Frankenstein (1873-1934), who composed the music for the official state song, "I Love You, California," saw a more ridiculous opportunity at Cooper's Camp in 1920. Trying to collect evidence for his divorce trial, he hired detective John McCaleb to make out with his wife Gertrude at the beach. He also had them followed by a witness, Fred J. Lee, who testified in court that "Mr. McCaleb put his head in her lap—or rather, she pulled his head down in her lap."

The following year saw 150 "beach cottages spring up like magic." These houses were mostly for vacation use, making them vulnerable to break-ins.

The Smiths—George (1874-1943), who managed the Philharmonic auditorium, and Caroline (1877-1970), who was the first female manager of the Los Angeles Philharmonic—had their beach house broken into every month for six months in 1922.

Deputy Sheriffs Archie Cooper and George Saunders (who also lived at the beach) thought they'd finally caught the culprits when they surprised four people dancing in the early morning hours: H. E. Gregg, A. E. Glencross, Evelina Cummings, and Jessie Courtney. However, the arrest turned out to be an embarrassment because Gregg was a police officer, and the Smiths had given him permission to be there. Incidentally, the Smiths were members of the Los Angeles Athletic Club, the future owners of Lower Topanga.

At another break-in, Archie and Saunders discovered 20 men and women at a table spread with food and "indications of something stronger than tea." This sophisticated "joy-riding party" was organized by 23-year-old F. S. Rubio of South Los Angeles, who fought with the deputies when they arrived.

The Cooper brothers romanticized the Wild West, and tried to recreate it on their Topango Ranch, which extended back into the Canyon. Therefore, they were more excited when the next group of people discovered their resort: cowboys!

> ...the famous Cooper's Camp north of Santa Monica, today boasts of an honest-to-goodness, rip-roarin' bunch of cow-punchers: also some of the niftiest cowgirls that ever wielded a

wicked six-shooter or roped a roarin' bronc'.

—"Topango Ranch Has Truly Western Color"
Santa Monica Evening Outlook, 1921-09-02

They were especially thrilled by cowgirl actress Rose "Helen" Gibson (1892-1977), who had brought along this posse to film her new Western. Archie proudly reported,

> She can ride high and fancy; bucking bronchos are her matutinal pastime and she can bulldog a steer as good as any man that ever flung a rope.
>
> —"New Movie Outfit Permanently at Topango Beach"
> *Santa Monica Evening Outlook*, 1921-08-30

Archie recalled a film shoot two years earlier, when "a famous English actress had to be lifted onto her pony for equestrian scenes." By contrast, Gibson brought a real rodeo culture that would later give the area the name The Rodeo Grounds.

Gibson's origins were unusual for a cowgirl. Born in Cleveland, Ohio, she'd been a city slicker until she was 17.

> During the summer of 1909, a real "Wild West" show came to Luna Park in Cleveland. Rose went to the show and took her girl friend.... [They] were enthralled with all the cowboys, Indians, bronc riding, bull dogging and girl trick riders. After the performance, they went down to the stable area... and asked how they could get a job with the Wild West Show....
>
> Rose took to her basic training as if she was raised on a horse.... But, Rose's girl friend... didn't qualify for the job.
>
> —*Helen Gibson: Silent Serial Queen* by Larry Telles
> (Bitterroot Mountain, 2013)

While working in rodeos, Gibson's signature tricks were picking up a handkerchief from the ground at full gallop, and riding a steer. She came to Venice with the Miller-Arlington Wild West

Show. After the 1911 season ended, the entire company was hired by Thomas Ince of the Inceville studio near Topanga Beach. Gibson rode her horse from Venice every day to perform tricks in Ince's Westerns, becoming film's first stuntwoman.

Gibson's first acting role was in *Ranch Girls on a Rampage* (1912), in which cowgirls visit a Venice amusement park and become so rowdy that they have to be chased out by police. The film was directed by Pat Hartigan and starred Ruth Roland, one year after they'd made *A Chance Shot* (1911) at the Topanga Beach Native American burial mound.

Gibson's greatest fame came from starring in *The Hazards of Helen* (1914-1917), the longest film serial in history with 119 episodes. She played a telegraph operator who turned into a kind of superwoman when problems arose, saving the day with incredible stunts like leaping onto moving trains, jumping motorcycles, and standing on galloping horses. The studio named her "Helen" after her character.

In August 1921, Gibson decided to make the Topango Ranch the permanent headquarters for her films, and began working on a Western with actors Bob Burns (1884-1957) and Jack Ganzhorn (1881-1956). Unfortunately, the financiers, IXL Productions, went bankrupt during filming and didn't pay the actors. Even worse, riding horses in the film irritated Gibson's recent appendicitis surgery and put her back in the hospital. Other studios saw that she was unfit and stopped hiring her. A difficult period followed, during which she had to sell all her possessions to survive.

The working title of her Topango Ranch film was *Going Some*, but the film appears to have been released by a different studio the following year as *Thorobred* (1922). It is one of the estimated 75% of silent films that are lost.

For the next five years, Gibson supported herself by performing at rodeos and Wild West shows again. When she returned to acting at age 35, she was only given small parts and stunts, yet she forged a career out of this that lasted until the 1960s.

One cowboy actor who remained at the Topango Ranch was Wallace Jones Willett (1898-1970), who went by "Jonesy" and doubled for star Ken Maynard (1895-1973). In July 1922, like a scene from a Western, Jonesy helped solve a crime by recovering a stolen safe from the bushes with two other Topango Ranch cowboys, Clarence Ditman and William "Red" Steeb (1885-1967). Bandits had pried open one side of the safe, then given up and thrown it away. Inside were several thousand dollars in stocks, bonds, and checks stolen from the Bellflower Post Office.

Jonesy would go on to become a rodeo calf roper, and the manager of the Orcutt Ranch above Northridge. Red's surname suggests that he was related to Olga Steeb, but I couldn't figure out how.

CHAPTER 11

The Sheriff Traeger Rodeo

The Topango Ranch's first official rodeo was thrown on August 27, 1922 by Archie Cooper, in honor of Sheriff William Traeger (1880-1935), and attended by 1,500 people.

Three world champions performed: trick rider Buff "Big Buffalo" Brady Sr., bronco rider Hank Potts, and Roman rider Benny Crawford.

Two 10-year-old children also performed: "Dolores Steelman, a small deaf and dumb girl who gave an exhibition of trick riding, and Newton House, who rode a calf."

Dolores (1912-1940), a fearless rodeo prodigy despite her handicap, was the youngest of 10 equestrian siblings.

Her father, actor Hosea Steelman Sr. (1876-1953), had a business supplying cowboys, horses, and props to Westerns. He worked on the first feature film ever made in Hollywood, *The Squaw Man* (1914), which was also director Cecil B. DeMille's first film. The two friends ended up working on 20 films together.

A barbecue featured goat and steer meat, and Archie contributed vegetables from his garden.

CHAPTER 12

The Elks Rodeo

Although rodeo stunts were introduced to the Topango Ranch by Helen Gibson in 1921, and the first official rodeo was thrown there in honor of Sheriff William Traeger in 1922, the Topanga rodeo truly flourished in 1923, when at least five rodeos were held.

The biggest rodeos were thrown by the Elks and Moose Lodges, two fraternal clubs that would have been present at the Traeger Rodeo, since he was a member of both.

On June 2-3, 1923, the Elks threw a two-day rodeo for the stated purpose of raising money to send their band to a convention at the Grand Lodge in Atlanta, GA. However, much more money must have been spent in preparing for this "monster rodeo."

Nearly 100 carpenters were employed to build the arena, grandstands, and "Days of '49" town.

> A regular frontier town will be built with all the necessary dance halls and gambling dens. The old fashioned bars will be much in evidence with all the old "kick" in everything but the liquid goods, but a tribe of dance hall girls will be there to make the merry makers forget that incident of ancient history.
>
> —"Elks of Entire Southland Coming to Topanga Beach Rodeo June 2–3"
> *Santa Monica Evening Outlook*, 1923-05-18

The rodeo's director, George C. Flores, was praised for organizing "the greatest line-up of real stars of the arena that has ever been brought together for a wild west show in Southern California." 50 champions, along with steers and wild horses, were selected from as far away as Oregon, Montana, and Wyoming.

Special attractions included the act of "Skeeter Bill" Robbins (1887-1933) and his wife Dorothy Morrell (b.1888), world-champion ropers and riders.

Multiple world champion "Tuck" Gibson rode Steamboat, "said to be the world's most famous trained bucker." Before the fence to the arena was completed, Tuck and Steamboat had an exciting practice ride that ended half a mile up the canyon. Heavy brush prevented cowboys from roping Steamboat, so Tuck had to hang on until the horse tired out.

Western actor Buck Jones (1891-1942) was appointed as one of the judges.

The food was prepared by "world's famous barbecue artist" Joe Romero (1852-1932). This East LA cowboy earned his reputation by cooking for around 5,000 people at a time, and catering around 25 events a year, for almost 50 years. His method of burying the meat in a pit of hot coals was a point of local pride for Angelenos, who looked down on grilling as suitable only for Boy Scouts. One of his specialties was a bull's-head breakfast, which fell out of fashion in the late 1920s.

"Virtually all of Southern California, be they Elks or not," attended the rodeo, including all the orphans and poor children of the Santa Monica Bay cities, who were invited for free. Special bus service was set up from Santa Monica, and the Elks donated their own cars to help transport "the largest crowd of people who ever witnessed a rodeo in these parts." Guests camped overnight on the beach to enjoy the two-day event.

> Thirty thousand people attended the Elks' round-up at Topanga canyon yesterday, the attendance passing wildest expectations....
>
> The road from Santa Monica to the show grounds was like

Broadway on a busy day....

Seating capacity for 25,000 people around the arena was soon filled to overflowing and thousands of spectators eager to see the show dotted the hills on all sides....

Six-guns, spurs, high-heeled boots and two-gallon hats were to be seen in all directions....

—"Crowd Is Estimated at 30,000"
Santa Monica Evening Outlook, 1923-06-04

The wild west arena is going to one of the most unique ever built. Due to the topography of the canyon it has been found possible to build a regular amphitheatre. The entire mountain side will be terraced and seats built to accommodate several thousand people.

—"Noted Cow-Girl Will Take Part in Rodeo"
Venice Evening Vanguard, 1923-05-31

This rodeo must have been the biggest event ever held in Lower Topanga.

CHAPTER 13

The New Bridge Rodeo

After the success of the Elks Rodeo, and with the infrastructure now in place, it seemed like every summer holiday or event at the Topango Ranch would be celebrated with a rodeo. "Bringing back the spirit of the wild west with… its lawlessness and its freedom" must have felt like the perfect remedy for the Prohibition, anti-gambling times. And since these rodeos were hosted by Deputy Sheriff Archie Cooper, and lightly policed by his friends Sheriff William Traeger and Deputy Sheriff Frank DeWar, the attendees probably got away with a lot.

On June 24, 1923, a rodeo was held to celebrate the opening of a new bridge across the Topanga Lagoon. The straighter route was part of the new Oxnard-San Juan Capistrano Highway, a clunky misnomer for an improvement that the Cooper brothers protested as unnecessary, since it cut right through their campsite only to stop at the Malibu gate. Nevertheless, the rodeo seemed to have been enjoyed by all, and Helen Gibson even returned to perform in it.

> Thousands of persons from Santa Monica and neighboring cities attended the barbecue and rodeo yesterday afternoon at Cooper's Ranch….
>
> Several long lines were formed by the rodeo visitors before the improvised tables where the barbecued meat and "frijoles" were served, while long benches fashioned after those used in

army camps were the dinner tables. Occasionally, wandering hungry mules stole up behind the dining folk and purloined food from the paper dishes. Coffee was served in ranch tincups of large capacity.

Local color also was added to the rodeo by the numerous stands which affected being operated as those of the days of '49.

Preceding the rodeo, there was an entertainment by dancing girls, while speakers representing Southern California Automobile club [Carl McStay], the State Highway commission [William H. Carter] and Los Angeles board of county supervisors [R. F. McClellan] were heard.

Spectacular horsemanship was shown, not only by the numerous "bukaroos," but by Grace Teed, Marrietta Gregory, Miss M. Carlson, Helen Gibson and Miss M. Steelman, all of Los Angeles....

Hank Steelman of Hollywood, Archie Cooper, Clarence Pittman, J. A. MacDonald, Noy Henry, Tex Grove, [Al] Brassfield, Clarence [Sovern], Slim Riley, "Whitey" [Sovern], Jim Hogan, Ben Corbett, Jim Shannon, Felix Luttrell, Milton Carter, Gene McCay and H. Bowman were among the cowboys. Most of the group reside in Los Angeles.

Music was furnished by the American Legion band of Hollywood. Several songs by Miss Hazel Devere, of Los Angeles, who has sung at club entertainments in Santa Monica numerous times, were applauded. She sang in front of the bleachers.

Judges of the rodeo were Zibe Morse, Ed Bowman and Art Manning. Valuable prizes were awarded by them to the winners of the various events.

—"Thousands Roll Over New Road"
Santa Monica Evening Outlook, 1923-06-25

This is the only Topango Ranch rodeo that Archie Cooper is known to have competed in.

Hank Steelman (1902-1939), who worked as a double for actress Mary Pickford (1892-1979), was the son of actor Hosea Steelman. "Miss M. Steelman" was probably also related.

Clarence Pittman was probably Clarence Ditman of the Topango Ranch, although I'm not sure which spelling is correct.

After the opening of the new highway, the name "Topango," suggesting a fantasy Wild West place, began to lose its mystique, and the mainstream "Topanga" was more often preferred. The Topango Ranch even changed its name to the Sea View Ranch.

CHAPTER 14

The Fire Rodeo

When the Cooper brothers threw their own rodeos, they hired Spanish chef Fred Ramirez to cater, resulting in numerous complaints about his dangerous fires.

On the Fourth of July 1923, Ramirez's barbecue seems to have accidentally ignited a brush fire.

> Scores of men attending a rodeo at Cooper's Ranch and many residents in the vicinity have been pressed into service and are fighting the flames.
>
> The flames started in back of Cooper's Ranch and veered toward Las Flores Canyon. A light breeze, however, drove the flames back on Cooper's Ranch, which is now threatened with destruction.
>
> —"Las Flores Canyon Is Fire Swept," *Los Angeles Times*, 1923-07-05

During this time, civilians could be "pressed into service" if a fire broke out near them. It was actually illegal to wait for firefighters. The 1933 Griffith Park Fire is still the deadliest fire in California history for this reason, with 29 civilian deaths, even though it only burned 49 acres.

The Cooper brothers were fortunate that their much larger fire took no lives or structures.

CHAPTER 15

The Moose Rodeo

On September 8-9, 1923, the Moose Lodge threw their own two-day rodeo. The best cowboys returned to compete for prizes, and there was an all-night dance in the beach pavilion with music by The Moose Orchestra. The American Legion Band of Hollywood also performed.

Joe Romero was again hired to barbecue, and cooked buffalo meat provided by Arizona cowboy Sam "Buffalo" Smith, the only owner of a buffalo herd in the Southwest.

Native American cowboy Miguel Severas from Sonora, Mexico, formerly a follower of Pancho Villa, challenged anyone in California to beat him to the $100 prize for the calf-roping contest. His rivals were Siciala Salinas (Topango Ranch), Henry Wertz Sr., and Henry Wertz Jr. (Globe Mills, CA).

Another rodeo performer was Archie's 14-year-old daughter, Edythe Cooper (1908-1982). She was billed as "the champion girl rider in the Southwest," with reports that "Miss Cooper's riding has long startled rodeo fans wherever she has appeared." Her title was challenged by Myrtle Gibbins of Shelby, MT, a last-minute entry in the women's stunt-riding event, but it's not known who won.

Archie's estranged wife Emilie (1891-1977) had finally divorced him in 1922, suing for alimony and accusing him of cheating with a woman named "Miss Belle."

Besides the usual events, the Moose Rodeo featured some

odder entertainments like a fat men's race and a midnight badger fight.

> Anyone who has ever seen Secretary [Dave] Hurley's famous badger in action will appreciate what a momentous occasion this will be.
>
> —"Loyal Order of Moose," *Los Angeles Times*, 1923-08-12

There was also a swimsuit contest/parade hosted by Mack Sennett (1880-1960), known for his short films of "Bathing Beauties," and a contest for "The Queen of the Moose." The Queen was feted with a "triumphal procession," and tickets were auctioned to ride in her chariot.

Attendance was in the thousands, and "[shattered] all records for a Moose festivity."

CHAPTER 16

The Tom Mix Rodeo

On September 30, 1923, Archie Cooper planned a rodeo party for the judges of Los Angeles Superior Court, perhaps to thank them for letting him off in the Arthur Valentine assault case earlier that year. The rodeo's co-host was Tom Mix (1880-1940), the most famous cowboy actor of the time, and also an Elk.

Mix may have starred in a Western that was shot at the Sea View Ranch earlier that month by the Fox Film Corporation, which he worked for. All that's known about this film is that an actor named A. M. Fenton was thrown from a horse and broke his shoulder. A fire destroyed most of the films produced by the Fox Film Corporation in 1937.

Despite its celebrity host, this rodeo was intended to be casual, with cowboys employed on the ranch performing. Fred Ramirez was again hired to barbecue, and slaughtered a buffalo for it. The night before the rodeo, Archie had Ramirez build a bonfire for the barbecue pit.

Deputy Fire Warden Mack J. Stanke saw the unsafe fire and ordered them to extinguish it. Archie argued the law, and the two men fought. Stanke was 50 lbs. lighter than Archie and disabled, but he was no one to mess with. He'd served on a destroyer in World War I, blowing up submarines off the Irish coast. Facing death daily, he'd had a nervous breakdown, and mangled his right hand. He'd come to Cooper's Camp to recover at the beach while living on government compensation. Ironically, Archie had helped him get his job, but some later resentment must have erased their friendship. Stanke dominated Archie in the fight. Afterwards, Archie retaliated by what we would call "swatting" Stanke.

> Deputy Cooper appealed to the Sheriff's office after the fight, and a squad of deputies responded.... Cooper declared that there was an insane man barricaded in a cabin at the ranch... and that he drew his gun and threatened to shoot people.
>
> —"Veteran Thrashes Deputy," *Los Angeles Times*, 1923-10-01

When deputies arrived, Stanke calmly went to jail, giving this account.

> Cooper had a fire, eight by fourteen feet, burning in a dangerous place. I told him that I would report him for violating the fire laws. He became abusive, threatened me and eventually struck me. We were then on my premises. I fought back and drove him out of my yard. He then shouted that I was under arrest. I told him that it would take a better man than him to arrest me and went in my house.
>
> He ordered out all his employees, armed them with guns and surrounded my house. Feeling tired, I went in and lay down. When the deputies came I surrendered to them. I have numerous witnesses to prove that I did not draw my gun, and that Cooper started the fight.
>
> —"Veteran Thrashes Deputy," *Los Angeles Times*, 1923-10-01

An official investigation into the incident sided with Stanke.

> I am satisfied that there were no grounds for Mr. Cooper's complaint of assault with a deadly weapon.... From the statements of numerous witnesses to the affair I conclude that Cooper was entirely in the wrong and was responsible for the fight.
>
> —"Beaten Deputy Resigns," *Los Angeles Times*, 1923-10-02

The African American community, which had decried the Los Angeles Superior Court's decision in the Valentine case, now saw Archie's beating by Stanke as divine justice.

> …an unerring judgment on this ferocious Cooper has come to pass and just a few days hence, he pounced upon a white man, and he got all that was coming to him, he got the beating of a life time, he got what he gave Valentine and then some, he has lost his job as Deputy Sheriff and truly in fact and in deed retribution for Arthur Valentine was at hand.
>
> —"Retribution," *California Eagle*, October 1923

Archie realized that he wouldn't be able to keep his job after attacking a White disabled veteran and immediately resigned, but protected his dignity by claiming that "the pressure of his business caused this action." He also said that he'd been contemplating the change for a long time, which was probably true, since Cooper's Camp had grown far beyond the campsite it was intended to be, involving the management of rodeos, restaurants, dozens of cabins, and a bathhouse. However, Archie didn't quit bullying Stanke. As soon as Stanke returned home from jail, Archie had him locked up again, this time in the General Hospital on a psychiatric hold.

Ultimately, Stanke was found to be sane, and Chef Ramirez was found guilty, but given a suspended sentence. Archie hired the same crooked attorney who'd helped him win the Valentine case, John L. Richardson (an Elk), and was somehow acquitted.

The rodeo went on without them. Tom Mix performed with his costar Tony the Wonder Horse. Edythe Cooper won a quarter-mile race and rode standing. Walter Lucore sustained bruises when he crashed into a wire fence, sadly breaking his horse's neck. Several judges entered the events. Philip Memoli led a Boy Scouts band. The audience was estimated to be 2,500.

CHAPTER 17

The Bullfight Rodeo

On the Fourth of July weekend of 1924, the Cooper brothers tried to top the successes of the Elks and Moose Rodeos with "one of the biggest rodeo programs ever attempted," a four-day event that would include bullfighting, for which they claimed to have obtained a special permit.

"Scores of Mexico's most prominent picaderos, toreadors and matadors [were] chosen to furnish thrills for the spectator." The star was Refugio "El Cuco" Hernandez, advertised as the most popular bullfighter in Spain. Two weeks earlier, El Cuco had become a local hero by saving a man's life when a bull broke loose during filming at Ince Studio, now located in Culver City. The film may have been *The Siren of Seville* (1924).

Bud Crone, a well-known Wild West circus performer, contributed "hundreds of his tempered bronchos along with scores of other animals" to the rodeo.

However, bullfighting was bound to be controversial. Miriam Brase, of the Santa Monica Bay Humane Society, warned the Cooper brothers that it was impossible to get a permit to wound an animal. On the afternoon of July 4, she showed up with four deputy sheriffs and had the rodeo shut down.

No bullfighting was happening when Brase arrived, but she had heard rumors that the fights were taking place at a secret location for a select clientele. Since the rodeo had started on July 3, it's possible that some bullfights really did happen.

It's also possible that the bullfights were never intended to hurt the bulls. A year earlier, El Cuco had fought a bull in Tulare, CA, following special rules laid down by the event organizers: "The toreadors will be unarmed and will rely solely upon their agility to escape. Bloodshed is not a feature of the show."

After the Bullfight Rodeo was shut down, no further Wild West events were planned, and the Topanga Beach rodeo era came to an end.

That same year, Miller Cooper started the Sea View Ranch Riding Academy, presumably to capitalize on his ranch's new fame. The instructor was H. J. Porter from London, who had previously instructed Canada's Royal Northwest Mounted Police. However, Miller's riding academy was short-lived.

In August 1924, a classified ad sold off the dance pavilion that had been the first success of Cooper's Camp.

CHAPTER 18

The Great Eleven Cult

An unusual Topanga Beach sight in August 1924 would have been 18-year-old Sam Rizzio (b.1906) walking back and forth, repeating, "I am a dead man," while a woman sprinkled a vial to wet the sand under his feet.

Sam was being converted to The Divine Order of The Royal Arms of The Great Eleven, the mysterious religion of his new wife Ruth Wieland (1899-1978) and mother-in-law May Otis Blackburn (1881-1951). The ceremony was intended to break him away from his old beliefs.

Ruth and May had created The Great Eleven religion after failing to find success in Hollywood, despite starring in and producing Portland's first feature film, *A Nugget in the Rough* (1917). They'd moved to Los Angeles in 1918, but by 1922, Ruth was supporting them by working downtown as a "taxi dancer," the early 20th century's less risqué version of a lap dancer, and sometimes an audition before prostitution.

That's when Ruth and May said that the biblical Angel Gabriel had appeared to them, telling them that he would help them write a book called *The Sixth Seal*, whose publication would bring about the end of the known world.

> They had been taken to a spot outside of Bakersfield, where just below the surface of the earth they were shown huge stores of golden nuggets and precious stones—which board was to be

> theirs upon the presentation to the world of the Sixth Seal.
>
> The Royal Family of the Chosen Eleven was to consist of nine "queens" and Ruth and May. For each "queen" a marble palace was to be erected on the "Mount of Olives" [Barnsdall Park] in Hollywood, and each "queen" was to be supplied with eleven "kings" chosen by the Angel Gabriel. The "queens" and their respective entourages were to rule the world with the advent of eternal life.
>
> —"Angel Gabriel Girls Quizzed," *Los Angeles Times*, 1925-02-07

While this was the gospel that the women preached, their religion was really about promising greedy people access to the mythical treasures if they would invest now in the production of *The Sixth Seal*, and about doing whatever Ruth and May said, no matter how irrational, because the angel had told them it was needed to bring the universe into harmony.

Sam had only known Ruth a short time when he married her in May 1924 and moved into her religious cult's headquarters, where Koreatown's MaDang Mall is today. He soon grew tired of the fanaticism he saw there, and begged Ruth to run away with him. During one argument, he supposedly hit her so hard that he drew blood, causing the cultists to form a wall around their queen. However, most accounts of what happened within the cult should be questioned because they come from Ruth and May themselves, who were deranged liars.

After the fight, Ruth said that Sam had abruptly packed his things and left. She told Sam's mother that he was doing religious work as penance, and would return when it was done. Later, she spookily phrased it as, "he is now a high priest, invisible to less spiritual eyes." To corroborate her story, she showed a short letter that she'd received from Sam.

> I am sorry that I have been so mean to you. I should have realized that after so many years of hard work that you have had in

> writing the Sixth Seal and the great sacrifices you have made that you were not strong and able to stand my abuse. This is good-by.
>
> —"Threats Sent Cult Accuser," *Los Angeles Times*, 1929-10-08

The irony of Ruth and May basing their religion around writing a book is that they were bad writers, afflicted by the same lack of subtlety as Sam's dubious letter. One of the few people privileged to have seen a draft of the *The Sixth Seal* called it "the most astounding, bewildering hodge-podge of biblical and mythological references," which is probably why its release was constantly delayed, and then never happened. In 1936, May would finally publish their only book, *The Origin of God*, which was similarly flawed.

> ...there is a lot of repetition that the author insists is necessary to really pound home her point, though a cynic might observe there are so few ideas that the repetition's real purpose was to generate enough material for a book.
>
> —*Cult of the Great Eleven* by Samuel Fort (Nisirtu Publishing, 2014)

Sam's younger brother Frank Rizzio (b.1909) immediately suspected that the letter was a forgery. He decided to do his own snooping, and infiltrated the cult by getting May to hire him as her chauffeur. When, after only a few days, he discovered Sam's clothes and suitcase, May tersely responded, "Well, maybe Sammie is coming back."

The Rizzios never went to the police, perhaps because they were trying to escape their own criminal past. Sam had already served nine months in juvenile hall for altering checks, and his father had been wanted for a triple homicide in Chicago in connection with a Black Hand gang, a precursor to the Mafia.

Sam's disappearance would only be properly investigated five years later, when Ruth and May were arrested for defrauding their followers. Handwriting analysts reviewed his letter and noticed that the word "sacrifices," of all things, was misspelled in the same way as in Ruth's own writing. They also determined that a second letter, sent to Sam's mother, couldn't have been written by him because he was left-handed.

The 1929 trial was the first time that the public learned about Sam's Topanga Beach ceremony. According to a pharmacist in the cult, May had revealed that the angel wanted them to kill Sam with a poison "which cannot be detected in the body of a drowned man," but said not to worry because Sam would be resurrected after *The Sixth Seal* was published. A few weeks later, May said that Sam only needed to die a symbolic death by walking on the poison. The pharmacist told police that she'd given May a vial of colored water in fear… but perhaps she lied, and perhaps May's angel changed his mind again.

While Frank was still working as May's chauffeur, he noticed the disappearance of another teenager in the cult, 16-year-old Willa Rhoads (b.1908). May told him that Willa had gotten a teaching job in Altadena. Others said that she'd gone east to marry.

During the 1929 police investigation, Willa's parents broke down and confessed that she was dead, revealing one of the cult's darkest secrets. According to their story, May had summoned them from Portland in November 1924 to install Willa as one of the 11 queens who would rule the world from Hollywood. Upon her arrival, an excited Willa was gifted seven puppies named after the seven syllables in solfège: Do, Re, Mi, Fa, Sol, La, Ti. On Christmas Day, she developed a tooth infection, but her parents refused to take her to a doctor. Instead, they told her that she would die and be resurrected, which Willa apparently accepted. She died on New Year's Day.

To ensure Willa's resurrection, May laid the body on ice and preserved it in salt and spices. Then she ordered the same thing for Willa's puppies, which had to be poisoned first, saying that they would help Willa awaken at the seven notes of the Angel Gabriel's trumpet.

Willa and the puppies were kept frozen for more than a year, requiring deliveries of 600 lbs. of ice a week. In addition, the cult moved three times with the frozen bodies, one of their headquarters being the future site of Santa Monica's trendy Urth Caffé.

In February 1926, May said that Willa's resurrection wasn't going to happen as soon as she'd thought, and told Willa's parents to bury the bodies under the floorboards of their Venice home. Police found Willa and the puppies there in 1929.

May explained that Willa had been "sacrificed to save the world," making it sound like she'd planned Willa's death. The summons to Los Angeles, the gift of the puppies, the sudden illness, and the portentous dates also suggest this. Willa was even reported to have been feeling better on New Year's Eve, and celebrated with the cultists, before her sharp decline the next day, as if poisoned.

For that matter, was it a coincidence that Sam Rizzio had been hastily brought into the cult only to disappear like Willa? Was it a coincidence that they were close in age, and that their disappearances happened within months of each other?

In February 1925, a small metal box was found at a construction site in Topanga, near Fernwood. It contained photos of May with a wealthy Portland businessman named Fremont Everett, financial papers showing gifts amounting to $100,000, and old love letters. This discovery forced May to admit that she'd had an affair with Everett and buried their correspondence six years ago, after he'd refused to leave his wife.

During the 1929 trial, May admitted to digging the box up herself. The significance of this publicity stunt is said to be that she needed to show where her money was coming from because police already suspected her of defrauding her followers. The affair would naturally be denied, and the involuntary outing of gifts might make them seem more believable. Everett did deny the affair, and said that he'd only met May to buy property from her. He pointed out that she'd also been married at the time, and described any letters they'd exchanged as strictly business, which might explain why some were written on company stationery.

Although it's believed that May really did have an affair with Everett (and possibly blackmailed him), my theory is that she added forged letters to their business correspondence to make it appear that way. Everett's love letters are written in the same utilitarian language as Sam's letter.

> I have loved you for eleven years. It is my desire and intention to ask you to become my wife as soon as I am free.... For value received I have given you notes amounting to $25,400.
>
> —"Plow Reveals Romance," *Los Angeles Times*, 1925-02-12

This letter also seems to be influenced by numerology, a major concern of The Great Eleven. The number of years the affair lasted is 11, and the numbers in the gift amount are 2 + 5 + 4 + 0 + 0 = 11.

Furthermore, the first sentence of Sam's letter has 11 words.

One year before her arrest, May traveled with nine followers to Stovepipe Wells in Death Valley to perform a ceremony. Although no details are known, it is believed that she equated the wells with "the bottomless pit" in the Book of Revelation. Police later investigated rumors that Sam's body was disposed of there. A trip with 11 travelers would make more sense.

A few months before her arrest, May ordered Willa's father to bury a large trunk at Big Bear Lake without telling him what was inside. Police again suspected that it was Sam's body, but they never found the trunk.

Ruth and May's arrest happened while the cult was living in the Simi Hills on a 164-acre compound (1 + 6 + 4 = 11), which the press sarcastically dubbed Harmony Hamlet. Cultists had been told to drive their cars into the wilderness and leave them to rust as a sign of their devotion. More animal sacrifices occurred there, and perhaps human sacrifices too, since people kept dying and disappearing. May's plan to build refrigerated warehouses to store dead bodies for resurrection added to suspicions.

In 1929, Ruth and May were charged with grand theft. The charges against Ruth were dropped, but May was sentenced to a minimum of eight years in 1930. She appealed, claiming that stories of Sam and Willa had been improperly admitted to frighten the jury, and had nothing to do with whether she'd committed theft. In 1931, a judge agreed with May and let her go. Remarkably, Ruth and May were never charged with any of the deaths or disappearances in their cult, which continued to exist for many years afterwards.

There are a few surprising similarities between The Great Eleven and The Charles Manson Family. Both had leaders who wanted Hollywood fame and felt rejected. Both had a presence in Topanga. Both sought out the Book of Revelation's "bottomless pit" in Death Valley. Harmony Hamlet and Spahn Ranch were only a few miles apart in the Simi Hills.

Sam Rizzio's disappearance remains unsolved.

Was he poisoned? Was he drowned? Was he frozen?

Is he buried in Topanga? Death Valley? Big Bear? Under someone's floor?

The next dark secret of The Great Eleven is waiting to be revealed.

CHAPTER 19

Athletic Club, Hearst Want Topanga Yacht Harbor

In September 1924, the Los Angeles Athletic Club bought 1,800 acres of beach property from the Title Insurance and Trust Company with the intention of building a Topanga Yacht Harbor, a beach club, and subdividing the rest of the land among themselves. The sale was facilitated by members General Moses Sherman (1853-1932) and Eli P. Clark (1847-1931), both instrumental in creating the Hollywoodland development one year earlier.

In July 1925, William Randolph Hearst (1863-1951) got involved, buying (or buying an interest in) 3,400 acres of the historic Rancho Boca de Santa Monica that included Topanga Beach. The Rancho's remaining 2,000 acres were bought by friends of Hearst.

Hearst kept his intentions secret, but he was said to be "heavily interested" in the Topanga Yacht Harbor project, which was actually planned to be below Parker Mesa. He was working with LAAC Vice President Frank A. Garbutt (1869-1947), who'd come up with the idea. Garbutt owned one the first major yachts in Southern California, the 90-foot Skidbladnir, which he'd named after a magical ship in Norse mythology.

Hearst is blamed for giving out five-year land leases, allowing residents to become more established, and newcomers to build more homes. The LAAC reluctantly became landlords, which presented an obstacle to their development plans.

Hearst also bought property in Tuna Canyon, which was rumored to be for a movie studio. Other rumors that Tuna Canyon was the first proposed site for Hearst Castle ring false, since he'd already started building his castle in 1919.

Around this time, LAAC President William May Garland (1866-1948) accomplished his goal of getting Los Angeles selected as the host for the 1932 Summer Olympics.

The LAAC's attention suddenly shifted away from constructing the Topanga Yacht Harbor to preparing for the Olympics, while completing other projects already underway like the Maple Ranch Gun Club near Bakersfield (1925), the Riviera Country Club in Pacific Palisades (1927), and acquiring the Pacific Coast Club in Long Beach for another yacht harbor (1928).

The LAAC had hoped to increase their Topanga property's value by operating the only yacht harbor in the bay, but were disappointed when Santa Monica began planning its own harbor by the Pier in 1926, and eventually built it in 1934.

Also in 1926, the widowed Rhoda May Rindge (1864-1941) began losing the fight to keep her Malibu Ranch private when the State seized part of her land to build Roosevelt Highway. In 1927, the Malibu Colony was the first part of the ranch to open to the public, taking away from Topanga Beach's allure as the end of the road.

The LAAC loved polo, building no less than four polo fields at Riviera. In November 1929, they started building one at Topanga Beach too, presumably on Shady Lane, where the prison camp had been.

That same month, their California Yacht Clubhouse in San Pedro burned down. Attention again shifted away from Topanga developments. The Great Depression, which had started one month earlier, would further limit the LAAC's spending.

The LAAC's proudest moment came when all their planning for the Olympics was rewarded with 49 medals, including a gold in yacht racing. This was a huge boost to the US, which won the

Olympics with 103 medals total. By comparison, Italy came second with 36 medals.

Amazingly, the unforeseen delays to building a Topanga Yacht Harbor, which the LAAC encountered from the start, continued for 77 years. During that time, they were constantly trying to evict the tenants, and pursue their original plan or other developments... and if there had been one less obstacle, they probably would have succeeded. After the Great Depression, it was World War II. And by the 1950s, the residents were so deeply rooted that they sued the LAAC to stay another 15 years. As a result, Topanga Beach remained in limbo until State Parks bought it in 1971 (and made it public in 1979) to block future developments.

Lower Topanga, the first two miles of the Canyon, was bought in 2001, but has actually remained in limbo until the present (2020, almost 100 years!) while the State waits for money to turn it into a park.

CHAPTER 20

The End of Cooper's Camp

As Topanga Beach fell into limbo, bootleggers sensed a lack of oversight and grew bolder.

In January 1925, Deputy Fire Warden H. D. Smith encountered a gang waiting for a midnight rum ship by an empty cabin. The gang beat him with a club, and left him lying in the sand overnight.

An investigation by Archie Cooper and Deputy Sheriff William Edward Harris turned up a description of one of the suspects, a dark-skinned man in a blue serge suit. The getaway car was described as a gray Studebaker with a white stripe. But could these stereotypical gangland descriptions have been fabricated to hide a sketchier story?

Later that year, Smith and Harris (an Elk) were themselves arrested for running a speakeasy out of a "lunchroom" called the Rustle Inn at the entrance to Topanga Canyon.

> Topanga beach establishments have been operating for some time, and… it has been the custom of the operators to bring up many gallons of illicit liquor to the place early Saturday, which has served as refreshments over the week-end.
>
> —"Canyon Raid Disastrous to Deputies"
> *Santa Monica Evening Outlook*, 1925-08-17

A photo from this time shows that the facade of the Rustle Inn was painted with a large ad for Eastside, an East LA near-beer that was popular during Prohibition because it squeaked just under the 0.5% alcohol-by-volume (ABV) limit.

The Cooper brothers were not implicated in the raid but surely knew what was going on. They must have advised the defendants to hire Howell W. Richardson, the younger brother of their attorney John L. Richardson (who had died in a landslide in Kern County one month earlier). The defendants were found guilty.

In September 1925, Miller and Mary M. Cooper hosted the wedding of their oldest daughter Edna to Alfred Jackson Sutton (1897-1955) of Metro-Goldwyn Studios. Their middle daughter, Sarah, was the maid of honor, and their youngest, Mary Laurania, was the ring bearer. The wedding was a joyous respite before 1926 arrived with back-to-back disasters.

Early in the morning on January 3, 1926, a fire started in an empty beach cabin and spread in both directions. No lives were lost, but the bathhouse belonging to Alfred Patterson Stewart (b.1874) and 10 cabins burned, and the dance pavilion was damaged. The cause of the fire was not discovered, but Sylvester Elliot (b.1897) of Topanga was arrested. Closer scrutiny revealed that this beach watchman had pretended to be a federal officer in order to get his job, and that he was writing bad checks.

Then, in February 1926, two weeks of storms brought hail and "mountainous waves" that destroyed a Greek fish market and 14 cabins. "Swirling wreckage was hurled with battering-ram effect against standing cabins that dropped like card houses." A story was told of two women who had rushed all the belongings from one's cabin into the other's, only to have misjudged which cabin would survive. (In 1927, another storm wiped five more cabins off the beach.)

Even more tragic were the deaths of two men who were repairing a pier at Inceville when their boat capsized in the storm: Thomas Compton of Santa Monica, and Harry Hoover of Topanga. Lifeguards Jimmie O'Rourke and Allen B. Law rescued two other men who'd been in the boat, resuscitating them in the fake

European church on the beach, left over from an Inceville movie set.

The destruction must have devastated the Cooper brothers' business because they left Topanga Beach soon afterwards. However, more hardships followed them.

Miller and his wife moved to Paso Robles, where their daughter Sarah died at age 19 in November 1926 "after an unsuccessful effort to save her life by an operation"... perhaps from a car accident? Many of Sarah's former Santa Monica High School classmates attended her funeral.

Archie moved to Mint Canyon, near Santa Clarita, where he got involved with a widowed sculptor who had a restaurant, a 1,600-acre ranch, several children, and two names: Mrs. Vera Sharp and Mrs. De Font. In August 1927, this interesting but unethical woman was accused of stealing clothes and silverware from a neighbor's house. She and Archie were also accused of stealing a cow and barbecuing it for her restaurant. It would seem that after years of bad behavior, Archie had finally sunk to being a common criminal.

He had a brief success when he opened the Sunset Riding Stables in South Los Angeles, which became the Huntington Riding Stables in South Pasadena in 1929, but went bankrupt a year later.

Living in Burbank in 1931, he married a German-speaking Polish woman named Edwina Trusiewicz (b.1881). However, his life was cut short when he died in 1932 at age 49 of a ruptured appendix.

After the Cooper brothers left Topanga Beach, their resort was taken over by a Scottish widow named Lillian Fields (1883-1941), the same woman who later ran Elkhorn Camp.

In 1928, Cooper's Camp became the Topanga Beach Auto Court, and was managed by J. C. McGray.

CHAPTER 21

Bootleggers Shoot It Out

The raid on William Edward Harris and H. D. Smith's speakeasy in 1925 did not break up the bootlegging ring, as was claimed, because one year later "higher-ups" John W. Yeuk (1874-1946) and his wife Elizabeth (1876-1943) were arrested for selling whiskey.

Yeuk, who went by York, had been living at Topanga Beach since at least 1923, when he was arrested for "disturbing the peace" in Santa Monica. He was also arrested at the speakeasy raid, but apparently not recognized then as the kingpin.

In 1932, a fire burned two cabins he owned on Topanga Canyon Lane. It started in the cabin that York rented to L. W. Medina when wind blew embers from the fireplace into the drapes. Even though it was pouring rain, the cabin burned to the ground. The fire went on to damage the homes of York and film electrician Thomas P. "Teddy" Santee (1905-1963), who'd been arrested at the speakeasy raid, and to burn part of the hillside. Assistant Fire Warden Thomas Cheney (1889-1959), the older son of Topanga pioneer Columbus Cheney, suffered an eye injury when he slipped on a roof and fell face first into the stream of a high-pressure hose.

A less significant arrest was made of two men passing out "moonshine" at The Yellow Cab Company's beach picnic in May 1927. The cabbies' two-day party is worth mentioning anyway because of its parade of decorated taxis and its swimsuit contest for the girls in the office.

However, things turned violent in February 1928 when three

"rum-runners" were surprised unloading liquor from a speedboat early in the morning. Officers sprang from a hiding place in the rocks to arrest them, but quickly dove back behind the rocks to escape "a hail of bullets." A. B. Clift, 37, and Allen C. Smith, 29, were captured, but the third man escaped in the speedboat.

Around this time, Topanga Beach gas station owner Clayton Rust (1886-1974) and Greek fisherman John Foundoukos (1894-1969) benefited from a foiled bootlegging plot when they discovered three barrels of whiskey floating offshore after a storm. The Topanga Lane neighbors secretly brought the barrels home.

In January 1929, three other Greek fishermen, Spere Aneme (b.1884), Christ Yianulis (b.1895) and Mike Leonis (b.1892), made an unexpected discovery two miles offshore when they found a 20-foot basking shark in their net. They fought with the shark for four hours, almost swamping their boat before making it back to Topanga Beach. Hundreds of drivers stopped to look at the nearly 3,000-lb. shark in amazement.

In June 1929, a new Justice of the Peace, John L. Webster (1875-1962), was determined to rid Malibu of its reputation as a hideout for bootleggers. He was particularly upset by a recent raid on Topanga Lane, where residents had been kept up by "the offensive carousal of a liquor party." Three men had been arrested, and brought before him at "the ghostly hour" of 2:30 a.m., which reportedly sent Webster "over the top in a war against peace disturbers who make the nights hideous with hilarious liquor parties."

Other criminal activity included a "Possum Bandit" who played dead in the road to get drivers to stop. In 1926, in the Pomona area, the Possum Bandit managed to scare all his victims away by jumping up too quickly to rob them. In 1927, he tried again at Topanga Beach, but the people he intended to stop were spooked because of the late hour, and drove around him instead. They reported the sighting at the nearest telephone, but the Possum Bandit was gone when deputy sheriffs arrived.

In 1929, the Possum Bandit (or a copycat) did finally rob

someone in Los Angeles. This time he teamed up with a gunman, who hid behind a telephone pole, and they made off with the driver's car and wallet.

A crime with a twist happened on February 5, 1928.

Courtney Worthington, 20, and Margaret McDonald, 17, went for a drive up the coast with double-daters Rupert Duncan and Loretta Burger, both 17. They were forced to stop at the Topanga intersection after something popped two of their tires. While the boys made the repairs, the girls went for a walk on the beach.

The girls never returned, and after searching for two hours, the boys reported them missing. Speculations ran wild. Had they drowned? Had they been kidnapped? Had they run away, even though their parents could think of no reason why they would?

Search parties were sent into the hills and along the beaches. People began calling in with tips. A passing driver said that he'd seen the girls being stopped on their way to the beach by a man in a "large roadster." A taxi driver said that he'd driven the girls and two men from a Silver Lake apartment to a street corner in Glassell Park, where the girls lived.

The strangest part was when Police Lieutenant William L. Fore and one of his officers accepted the help of mystic Sidney R. Deacon (1860-1952) and his "mysterious wand for finding lost persons." Deacon's invention was "composed of 10 or 15 tiny tubes of different lengths," and supposedly could locate hidden minerals and oil as well. Millionaire Joseph Hemmel came along for support, assuring Fore that Deacon had once found his wife all the way in San Diego during a test of the wand's powers.

To make the wand work, Deacon had to wear the shoe of one of the lost girls on his left foot. Fore swore that when Deacon put the shoe on, the wand "quivered and strained in the inventor's hands as on a leash." After three hours of wandering around the beach, the group ended up at the nearly finished mansion that Austrian businessman Leon Kauffman (1873-1935) was building for his wife Clemence (1886-1932) to fulfill her dream of having a castle by the sea. Today, the Villa Leon, above the entrance to the Getty Villa, is a coastal landmark.

The Kauffmans weren't home, but Hemmel knew Leon, and called to get his permission to enter with a caretaker. Deacon then led the group into the kitchen, where the wand pointed insistently at the stove. They opened the stove and found… nothing.

On February 8th, the missing girls were found safe in San Pedro. When Fore called Deacon to tell him how far off he'd been, Deacon pondered for a moment, then suddenly remembered that his belt buckle was made of the same ornamental metal that was on the Kauffmans' fancy stove. He took off his belt and assured Fore that his wand was now pointing to San Pedro (but he didn't say if he was still wearing the girl's shoe). Deacon begged Fore to let him prove his invention in the next missing person case, but Fore never called him again.

Police found the girls in a room at the Maryland Hotel with three men, one of whom had secretly tipped off Burger's father about her location. Moving between hotels under fake names in Los Angeles, Bell, Watts, and now San Pedro, the girls confessed, with more giggles than tears, to having run away.

> [Courtney and Rupert] took too long to change the tires, so we walked to the beach. A couple of nice boys gave us a "lift" to Ocean Park. We went to a dance hall, and then home on a street car. There were lights in the house, and we were afraid to go in…. We got a kick out of seeing the kidnaping story in the papers.
>
> —"Two Kidnaped Girls Found in San Pedro"
> *San Pedro Daily News*, 1928-02-09

Another irresponsible youth who caused a scare was Charles Hudson, 20, a high school student body president, despite his college age. Coincidentally, he lived blocks away from the runaway girls in Glassell Park.

On May 5, 1928, Hudson's fraternity threw a full-moon party at Topanga Beach. A warm breeze blew, the ocean was calm, and the night was bright enough to see Catalina Island. Anchored just offshore, a white canoe glowed in the moonlight. Hudson felt a rush of adventure, and imagined that he could sail it to the island on a night like this. His classmates laughed, turning his reverie into a dare. Impulsively, Hudson retrieved the canoe, propped up a sheet of tin that he found on the floor, and sailed off.

The next day, after no word had come from Catalina or elsewhere, Hudson's classmates reported him missing. Fortunately, he was soon found safe on Point Dume. He described the ordeal that landed him there, after 13 hours in the water.

> I left the beach… about 11:30 o'clock Saturday night…. I got about 15 miles out and clouds hid the moon; then a heavy fog descended, the compasses went haywire, and all I could do was paddle….
>
> —"Youth Lands in Canoe at Point Dume, Will Try Catalina Again"
> *Santa Monica Evening Outlook*, 1928-05-08

Grateful to be alive, Hudson ached all over, and spent the next day in bed. "But I am not discouraged," he assured. "I am going to try again when I am 21."

Another newspaper quotes Hudson saying that he'd been planning the trip for six months, but how well-thought out could it have been if he left with someone else's canoe in the middle of the night?

I couldn't find evidence that he ever tried it again.

CHAPTER 22

Marmont Studio

A woman with red hair and "dancing brown eyes," Laura Way Mathiesen (1876-1966) opened Marmont Studio to sell her paintings in the first hairpin turn on the Topanga road on June 7, 1924. She wrote to her friends about it on stationery printed with an engraving of her studio and cabin.

> It is really a most wonderful location for I have at all times the variety of beach, rocky shore, palisades, mountain, cañon, or deep woods. In addition to this, all the world passes by my door. Sundays the traffic is almost intolerable. One day we counted sixty cars in ten minutes going in one direction but on other days it is not so bad.
>
> I wish you could see some of my work at the present time. I feel sure that it is getting better and better and I am almost surprised myself some of the time with my work on waves and rocks and ocean subjects, for I have so small a background of ocean experience. When first I tried it I felt really bewildered at the heaving, tumbling mass, but almost all the sketches I made that first week have been sold so I must have done tolerably well.
>
> And so the little studio idea came to me….
>
> —"Former Decatur Woman Has Mountain Studio"
> *The Decatur Review*, 1924-09-07

Marmont was probably Laura's wordplay on Montmartre, the

famous artists neighborhood in Paris. The name also combines Spanish words for "ocean" and "mountain," evoking the studio's location, and the main subjects of Laura's paintings. For what it's worth, Marmont Studio predated Hollywood's Chateau Marmont by five years. The "primitive and rough little house" in the Brookside neighborhood catered to weekend tourists, but was popular with locals as well.

> Marmont Studio, home of Mrs. Laura W. Mathiesen, well known California artist, is a gathering place for artists. Here on Sundays, particularly, they drop in to discuss their work, and to view Mrs. Mathiesen's paintings.
>
> —"Topanga Briefs," *Evening Outlook*, 1938-10-08

The Marmont Studio sign on the road read, "Painting and Pedigreed Pups," because Laura also ran a dog-breeding business there.

> If you dislike dogs, stay away from the Marmont studio, for some of the most charming wire-haired fox terrier puppies you ever saw are apt to enter informally at any moment.
>
> —"Wayside Studio Welcomes Rich Man, Poor Man, Child or Ancient to Its Doors," *Santa Monica Evening Outlook*, 1928-03-04

Laura felt a deep affection for her "live wires," and was so grateful when a man found her lost puppy Pango that she called him "A prince of good fellows, an uncrowned hero, a scholar and a gentleman." She also had a yellow cat named Caliph and a goat.

Laura's husband James L. Mathiesen (1879-1936) kept bees in the side canyon off the hairpin turn, and Laura painted designs on his honey-jar lids. When he became invalid for unknown reasons in the 1930s, she coped with the help of boarders like her sister Lucile Way (1877-1966), James's widowed mother Anna Mathiesen (b.1855), and a widowed clairvoyant named Frances Carre (1867-

1963), whose "gift of vision was internationally known." Frances was a preacher of the Bahá'í Faith, a Middle-Eastern religion that treats all major religions as one. Her son Earl Carre (1891-1943) also lived in the neighborhood with his wife and four children.

Laura was assisted by another mysterious character in taking over James's bee business.

> Just now I am interested in bee keeping, having about 60 hives which I am working with a most unusual partner, an exiled Russian Cossack. He is a man of many contradictions, who as a young boy entered the World war. The Russian revolution saw his property swept away, his family scattered. He is keenly appreciative of art, music, literature, speaks several languages, knows bees in a most scientific way....
>
> —"Russian Cossack Helps Artist in Her Bee Farming"
> *The Decatur Herald*, 1933-03-21

Laura herself was a person of many contradictions. She was an extrovert, but never painted people. She was known for her landscapes, but "her seascapes are even better." Her colors were "strong, yet restrained." Her style was between old and new.

> She is not a modernist in the accepted sense of the word, but she is decidedly not of the old school, and never loses her effects in overabundance of detail. She is quite willing to leave the individual leaf and blade to the imagination, though she seldom goes in for extremely broad effects....
>
> —"Wayside Studio Welcomes Rich Man, Poor Man, Child or Ancient to Its Doors," *Santa Monica Evening Outlook*, 1928-03-04

Laura was sure of her skill, yet she spent all her free time trying to improve: traveling to scenic places to paint, taking more art classes, and mentoring under famous painters like Walter Marshall Clute (1870-1915), Leonard Ochtman (1854-1935), and Frederick Oakes Sylvester (1869-1915).

> My work might be equal to the best of the California artists... an [George] Inness or a [Thomas] Moran or a William Wendt might be in your midst....
>
> —"Letters to the Editor," *Santa Monica Evening Outlook*, 1926-10-11

She was an elitist in her opinion that artists need formal art training, but egalitarian when it came to how art should be appreciated.

> On the theory that all people should have an opportunity to see and enjoy art for the asking, Laura Way Mathiesen has placed her rustic studio on the main highway in Topanga canyon, and the boy or girl on a hike into the wilds, the workman on the road, and even the passing vagrant are as welcome to come and enjoy her paintings as is the rich dowager who orders her chauffeur to park the shining sedan at the side of the road.
>
> Mrs. Mathiesen would rather see many of her paintings sold to poor people for small sums than to sell a few at prices asked by other artists. She paints because she loves to paint, and she wants the world to share in her own joy in her work....
>
> [She] has since made literally hundreds of landscapes of Southern California scenes... has exhibited in many Southern California galleries, but none of her paintings has ever been on display at an art dealer's store. She feels that this would make the price too high, and says that she will never sell in that manner.
>
> —"Wayside Studio Welcomes Rich Man, Poor Man, Child or Ancient to Its Doors," *Santa Monica Evening Outlook*, 1928-03-04

Even though Laura shunned the commercial art world, she complained about being overlooked. Meanwhile, she was widely admired, and became the vice president of the Santa Monica Art Association.

> Mrs. Mathieson [sic] is a painter in oils who has won much praise for her… [l]andscapes of beach scenes, beautiful canyon spots and ocean views.…
>
> —"Art Club Holds Usual Session in Canyon Home"
> *Santa Monica Evening Outlook*, 1926-05-24

Laura experienced setbacks when James died in 1936, and a brush fire burned down Marmont Studio in 1938, along with hundreds of homes in the Santa Monica Mountains.

"I lost everything except my paintings of Yellowstone. They were in the house and I grabbed them and ran." Later, she added that she had saved 70 "small sketches and studies covering her journey west."

Laura's journey began in Northfield, MN, where she was born Laura Rogers Way in 1876. Her grandfather had settled there after making a fortune in the California Gold Rush, and may have inspired her fascination with the West. She graduated in Fine Arts from the Pratt Institute in Brooklyn, NY in 1904. Afterwards, she worked as a Supervisor of Drawing (instructing both teachers and students) in public school systems in La Crosse, WI; Decatur, IL; Colorado Springs, CO; Butte, MT; and Oxnard, CA. Her biggest trip was to Europe, where she spent the summer of 1908 traveling from Scotland to Italy, covering long distances on foot.

Wherever Laura lived, she was at the center of society and the arts community. She was especially active in Decatur, where she painted sets for school plays, made shadow puppets for parties, judged baby contests, and gave talks on subjects like "Good Taste in Choice of Home Decorations and Furniture." She only lived there from 1905-1912, but she left such an impression that Decatur newspapers continued to write about her for decades, publishing some of the best accounts of her later life in Topanga.

Another important time for Laura was 1917-1922 in Butte, where she met James, a tire repairman who lectured on subjects like "Reincarnation" at the Theosophical Society. A new mysticism entered her life, and she began to express occult beliefs, like that thoughts can influence people and be photographed. Soon she was giving her own talks on "Telepathy" and the Hindu creation myth of "Hiranyagarbha." After marrying James in 1918, she quit teaching to work at the Theosophical Society, and regularly exhibited her paintings there.

Laura also became politically active in Butte. When women won the right to vote in 1920, she ran for local office as a Socialist. Years later, she joined the Malibu Democratic Club, and operated a polling place at her Topanga home.

Laura was able to continue living at Brookside after the 1938 fire with the help of the Red Cross, which built her a five-room house 100 yards off the road. She continued to use her home as an exhibition space, and again filled it "to the rafters" with a new Western series that included Mount Whitney, Mount Rainier, Pikes Peak, June Lake, Mono Lake, Death Valley, Palm Springs, Yosemite, and the giant sequoias.

In 1939, Laura married Gilbert Ruben van Alen (1869-1952), and took his Dutch Golden Age-sounding surname. Gilbert, an auditor for the city of Los Angeles, was probably too conventional for her, however, because their marriage ended.

In 1949, the *Los Angeles Times* came to interview Laura about a two-month road trip she'd taken alone to Zion National Park and the Grand Canyon.

> "You're never too old to do what you want to." These were the words of Laura Way van Alen, 73....
>
> "I am afraid of nothing...."
>
> She proudly displayed her paintings after apologizing for the condition of her house, explaining that in the morning she had canned 21 pints of pears and had company for lunch....
>
> When asked her opinion on modern art, Laura said, "Ha!" She enlarged on the subject by saying... "I realize some people like modern art. For me I like to see an object as God made it. I

don't think His type of art will ever be improved upon."

—"Woman Artist, 73, Enjoys Long Tour Alone in National Parks"
Los Angeles Times, 1949-09-11

Laura continued to travel, paint, and be active in the community until her death at age 90 in 1966. One of her favorite quotes, from a speech by Harvard President Charles William Eliot, wonderfully captures her: "To see beauty and to love it is to possess large securities for… [a happy and worthy] life."

CHAPTER 23

Spence's Cabins

In 1907, the newly widowed Keturah Catherine Spence (1857-1940) left Brantford, Canada, to start over in Los Angeles. Catherine, as she called herself, risked her fortune on an avocado orchard, becoming one of the first commercial growers in the US.

Just as avocado toast is a staple on today's menus, avocados quickly became part of the California lifestyle. The one perceived drawback was that English-speakers couldn't pronounce the original name, *ahuacate*.

The word "avocado" is a Los Angeles invention, selected at the Hotel Alexandria in 1915 by a group of farmers calling themselves the California Avocado Association, which surely included Catherine.

The success of Catherine's orchard allowed her to buy a house in present-day Koreatown, two building lots in San Diego, and to rent a house in La Jolla for the summer. She also became active in society as a member of the Scottish-expatriate Caledonian Club, since both of her parents were born in Scotland.

Catherine had already raised five children before coming to Los Angeles, some of whom followed her there.

Her son William McKay Spence (1879-1961) came in 1911, seeking a better climate to recover from an illness so severe that he'd lost a kidney. With his wife Florence (1883-1976) and children Frances (1907-1948) and Thomas (1910-1974), he moved into a house in Hollywood that Catherine bought for them.

At first, Florence worked at Bullock's department store in downtown LA. After William recovered, he got jobs as a telephone operator and a gas station attendant in downtown, and they had three more children: Marion (1913-2002), Howard (1915-1929), and Edna Mae (1920-2016).

Taking advantage of being at the center of early filmmaking, William and Florence turned their children into actors, with uncredited roles in *The Birth of a Nation* (1915), *Intolerance* (1916), and *The Cheerful Givers* (1917). Baby Howard's great talent, according to *Photoplay Magazine*, was his "wonderful repose."

In 1921, William's family rented one of the first vacation cabins at Topanga Beach. When the coast highway was raised for another lagoon bridge in 1933, it walled their Topanga Canyon Lane cabin into what became known as The Gulch, and later The Snake Pit.

In the late 1920s, Catherine somehow lost her orchard. To keep going, she sold the house that she'd bought for William, causing a rift between them, and forcing him to move his family to the beach cabin.

William's Topanga neighbors helped him find work in the area. Clayton Rust (1886-1974) hired him at his Topanga Service Station and Charles Potter (1882-1956) hired him at Potter's Store, both located at the Topanga intersection. William also got a job driving a bus, again probably with the help of Rust, a former bus driver. It may have been the Big Blue Bus, which started in Santa Monica in 1928.

However, the Spences weren't out of trouble yet. In 1929, they suffered their most devastating loss when 14-year-old Howard died from diabetes. That same year, the Great Depression began.

To restore stability, William created a motel business called Spence's Cabins by taking over the house next door, subdividing it into six units, and building an arched sign that joined the properties. He beautified the grounds with canna lilies and palms, and planted fruit trees to help feed his family like peaches, figs, bananas, and of course avocados... some of which were still being enjoyed by residents many decades later. For Depression-era meat, he raised rabbits because they bred quickly, and he could make a profit by selling some.

The children got through the hard time by focusing on school.

Edna Mae, in particular, immersed herself in activities at Madison Elementary School and Lincoln Junior High in Santa Monica. She played the Onion in a play about vegetables, helped recreate a Native American village, and managed a playground sports club. She was awarded certificates for her writing skills and her attendance record, not missing a single day or even being late for a whole semester. Later, she married a popular State Beach lifeguard and volleyball player named Nathan "Nate" Shargo (1910-2007), and moved to the Pacific Palisades.

Frances and Marion attended Willis Business College in Santa Monica. Later, Frances married Police Officer Ainsley Taylor (1901-1975) and moved to Beverly Hills, and Marion married contractor Tom Evans (1909-1984) and moved to Santa Monica.

Thomas studied art at Woodbury University in downtown LA, excelling at velvet paintings of cowboys, bullfighters, and island girls. At Topanga Beach, he fixed up boats he named "Topanga Belle" and "Popeye," and motored around the bay with his best friend Jake Fields (1913-1999), a talented sailor who already raced yachts in his teens. Jake's mother was Lillian Fields (1883-1941), who at different times ran Cooper's Camp and Elkhorn Camp.

In 1931, Thomas crossed paths with another young sailor named Frank Chapman, 22, who turned out to be a pirate. "The spirit of Old John Silver must have shuddered over [Frank's] clumsiness," however, because while trying to tow away a boat moored offshore, his own boat's propeller became tangled in fishing nets. Thomas saw Frank's boat spinning in circles, and not understanding the situation, he paddled out in a canoe to offer help. Frank asked to be taken ashore instead, and then ran away.

The fishermen were angry about their broken nets and called Malibu Constable Harland McNab (1888-1962), who "nabbed"

Frank farther on down the coast highway. It was later learned that Frank's "only known address was the Pacific Ocean," and that he'd stolen his boat in Wilmington two days earlier.

Thomas moved to his own cabin on Valley View Dr. in Topanga. He worked as a Big Blue Bus driver, and learned to fly planes in his free time. Later, he got a job at the aerospace company Northrop.

In 1936, Thomas married Roberta Robirds (1918-1998), a classmate of Edna Mae, and moved to Santa Monica. Roberta's distant cousins, Oby Robirds (1903-1967) and his partially blind sister Isabell (b.1908), had been neighbors of the Spences on Topanga Lane. Roberta made Thomas give up his pilots license after they had their first child, Beverly (b.1938), followed by Robert (b.1941), Richard (b.1943), and Donna (b.1948).

Beverly lives in Irvine today, and remembers visiting her grandparents at Topanga Beach. Part of the fun was being able to stay in one of the cabins. She enjoyed humming songs to Florence, who could quickly pick them up on the piano. In the backyard, she saw a clothesline being used to stretch rabbit skins. And walking along the creek to the beach, she was spooked by the water snakes in the lagoon.

Like many motels, Spence's Cabins attracted a few sketchy characters.

One was Horace Hurd (1917-1987), who got too drunk while celebrating his brother's arrival and began fighting with his wife Ann. Thomas tried to intervene, but was pummeled to the ground, while Beverly watched in horror. Fortunately, Thomas's injuries weren't serious, but Ann had to be taken to the emergency room for her elbow. Horace and Ann later divorced, yet Horace managed to rise from this low point to become a beloved sportswriter in Oregon known as "Red" Hurd.

Another problem tenant was Jacqueline Henninger, 34, who was stealing valuables from beach houses during parties. She was finally caught after she asked to use the phone of Louis L. Golden (b.1889), on Old Malibu Road, and left with his "17 jewel wrist watch." Her baffling denial of the theft was that she'd only taken the watch as a "keepsake."

In 1938, a major flood swept the area.

> Monday night numerous homes were flooded with several feet of water, but the worst damage centered at the Spence's cabins, which were swung completely around and half buried in deposits of sand and debris.
>
> —"Malibu Brevities," *Evening Outlook*, 1938-03-02

This was followed by two fires in the same year. The first was caught early when William rushed into the smoking house of Greek fisherman John Foundoukos (1894-1969) and rescued his housekeeper, who had fallen asleep with a cigarette. The second was the big Topanga fire, which damaged Spence's Cabins, and destroyed "nearly 50 homes and cabins at Topanga Beach."

Miraculously, by 1940, the Spence family was back on solid footing. According to Marion, William's business had grown to include 32 units, which suggests that he may also have been co-managing the Topanga Beach Auto Court with Swiss-born John P. Amacher (1895-1979), who later became a politician in Oregon.

Despite persistent threats—Foundoukos had to use his rowboat to rescue neighbors the Morgans from a flood in 1941, and cabins burned down in 1934 and 1949—Spence's Cabins endured until William retired in 1953. By then, he had become such a prominent community figure that he was seen as a kind of politician himself, and nicknamed the "Mayor of Topanga."

CHAPTER 24

Early Businesses

Around 1921, Clayton (1886-1974) and Ina Rust (1901-1988) moved to Topanga Beach. Nearly 20 relatives soon followed, making their family the biggest that ever lived in Lower Topanga. They not only influenced the development of that community, but of the local businesses, many of which they owned.

Although Clayton's first job in the area was driving a Santa Monica school bus, he soon became the operator of the Topanga Service Station at the intersection, where Oasis Imports is today. At first, it was just a shack with a single pump, but it quickly grew. By 1923, he was a distributor for Red Crown and had installed their signature red, white, and blue pumps. He must have done great business when the Elks, which he belonged to, threw their "monster rodeo" that year.

In 1936, a fire caused by bad electrical wiring burned Clayton's gas station, a garage he'd added, and a car that was parked inside. Topanga Fireman D. F. Hooper was burned on his hand and arm while fighting the blaze. The gas station was wisely rebuilt out of metal by Shell, but Clayton didn't like it as much, and sold it to neighbors Fred (b.1902) and Ethel Clark (b.1900). In 1949, Fred sold it to neighbors Henry "Van" (b.1910) and Thelma Van Ostrum (b.1912), who sold it to neighbors Roger (b.1930) and Jackie Sweet (b.1929) in 1951. It was demolished in the early 1970s, and rebuilt across the street by Gulf, then became GO-LO. Today, it's operated by ARCO.

Another early business was a small store across the street from the gas station that Clayton and his brother LeRoy "Roy" Rust (1893-1983) bought from Jack Messenger. Little is known about Messenger, but it seems like he was a cowboy from the Elks Rodeo who stayed on at Topanga. He isn't listed in the rodeo program, but the year before, he was touring California with three others who are: Hippy Burmeister (1894-1985), Calgary Jack McDonald, and Sam Howe. A fourth companion, Hank "Deadman"—so nicknamed because he once woke up in the morgue after being thrown from a bronco—was probably Hank Steelman (1902-1939) from the Elks Rodeo.

A store called Brigham Place, run by A. Brigham, also existed in the mid-1920s, but I couldn't determine if it was at this location.

The Rusts' store, run by Roy and his wife Blanche (1897-1967), was rebuilt as a narrow two-story building. On the second floor, the Title Insurance and Trust Company had an office.

In 1929, Roy and Blanche sold their store to Charles Potter (1882-1956), who had just moved to Topanga Canyon Lane. Mudslides from the hill in back became a problem, and in 1932 the tall building was pushed into a slant like the Leaning Tower of Pisa.

Potter rebuilt his store as a sturdier one-story building, but the rains of 1938 created a bigger mudslide that pushed it all the way into the street. He salvaged the lumber and rebuilt his store again, this time on the same side as the gas station, giving it the longer name Potter's Topanga Trading Post. Later, it became part of the Malibu Feed Bin.

Blanche's parents, Frank (1873-1944) and Myrtle Paxson (1875-1945), owned a hamburger stand called Paxson's Cafe at the future site of the Chart House and Mastro's Ocean Club. After they retired in 1939, it was renamed the Tides Cafe. It burned in 1941, and was rebuilt as Marinos' at The Point (later shortened to The Point) by a Greek family, who caught the restaurant's fish from long rowboats that they kept on the beach. Since 1933, Harry (b.1881) and Anna Marinos (b.1889) had been operating another

Topanga Beach restaurant simply called Marinos', where the Reel Inn is today.

The Greek fishing community at Topanga Beach can be traced back to Cooper's Camp. Their leader, Spere Aneme (b.1884), lived with John Foundoukos (1894-1969) and Mike Leonis (b.1892). Together, they opened a fish market of unknown name in 1923, which might have operated out of their cabin, because big waves destroyed both in 1926. (Their neighbor, "Greek George" Conios, had drowned on another high-surf day in 1920.)

The Greeks rebuilt their fish market, possibly an early version of Marinos', and re-opened with the help of two more friends: Lambros Hagis (b.1886) and Christ Yianulis (b.1895).

The De Long Cafe may have been related to these restaurants. I couldn't learn much about it except that it was started beside the lagoon in the late 1920s by Jess "Jack" De Long (1888-1953), a former Topanga grocer, and lasted until the 1950s.

On the north side of Clayton's gas station, Ina opened her own restaurant, called Rust's Barbecue, for the road workers who came to build the third bridge across the lagoon in the early 1930s.

In 1935, Ina began leasing her restaurant to others, including Louise Steeb (b.1914), who may created the next business there, the Topanga Inn. Louise lived on Old Malibu Road and was the daughter of William (1885-1967) and Frances Steeb (b.1892). William was an Elk who had been around since the rodeo days. In 1922, he'd worked as a cowboy on the Topango Ranch. In the mid-1920s, he'd had a restaurant called the Las Tunas Inn that was one of the only buildings on Las Tunas Beach to survive the stormy waves of 1926. Other restaurants he created were the Malibu Trading Post at Trancas Canyon in the early 1930s, and the Big Rock Cafe in the late 1930s.

On the south side of Clayton's gas station, Edward (1876-1964) and Minnie Shriner (1878-1964) opened Shriner's Wayside Stand in 1926, in the former Rustle Inn. They sold it in 1937 to Ina's friend Lucie Loggins (b.1893), who renamed it the Step Inn Cafe.

In 1938, a Swiss cook named Werner Etter (b.1901) sold the Step Inn Cafe to its longest owner, Sue Blackwood (1898-1962), who took it over in the same week that the 1938 flood happened. She endeared herself to the neighborhood by staying open all night to feed the rescue workers. Her brother Cecil Terrill (1902-1972), sister Florence Zollner (1894-1968), sister-in-law Montana Terrill (1903-1982), and Montana's sons Steven (b.1924) and Howard Terrill (1929-2019) helped run the restaurant. During World War II, Sue married Howard Van Wagner (b.1908), another "Van" for short, who also got involved.

The Step Inn Cafe was made famous as the place where Kirk Douglas (1916-2020) breaks the heart of Ruth Roman (1922-1999) in the 1949 film *Champion*. It burned on July 4, 1958, but was rebuilt as Ted's Step Inn Cafe by Sidney "Ted" Koskoff (1908-1992) of Ted's Grill in Santa Monica Canyon. In 1962, a new owner, Irene Girourd, renamed it French's Wee Nook. It was demolished in the late 1960s.

Besides contributing to the development of Lower Topanga, both Clayton and Ina were connected to some of the region's early settlers.

Clayton grew up in Stillwater, OK, but spent the best time of his youth leading tour groups on mules into the Grand Canyon. In the early 1910s, he and several others of his family came to Los Angeles.

In 1913, Clayton got a job as a surveyor for the Topanga road that was being rebuilt, and married his first wife May Jennie Daic (1887-1915), the daughter of a Calabasas pioneer named Wencil Daic (1846-1934). Clayton also befriended Malibu pioneer Rhoda May Rindge (1864-1941) and Topanga pioneers the Cheneys. In 1915, the same year that the new road was completed, May Jennie died at only 28.

For the next five years, Clayton worked as a car mechanic in Northridge. He met Ina, who was nearly half his age, while living at the Burbank boarding house of her aunt, Senea Lou Barnes

(1865-1946). Senea had come to California with nine children after her husband died in Texas in 1902. She was preceded by her brother Josiah Thrasher (1867-1943) and his wife Alice (1878-1906), Ina's parents, who were pioneers of Van Nuys. Alice was said to be related to Jerome C. Davis (1822-1881), the founder of Davis, CA, but I couldn't figure out how.

In 1919, Clayton and Ina married, and he got a job at the Orcutt Ranch above Northridge. Soon afterwards, he got a job running the Lower Topanga gas station.

The Rusts first lived in a small beach house, then bought a two-story house behind Cooper's Camp. They were able to afford it because the builder had run out of money before finishing the interior. The Rusts couldn't finish it either, and only lived on the first floor.

A few houses away lived Greek fisherman John Foundoukos (1894-1969), whom Clayton befriended.

Some of the first relatives to move to Lower Topanga were Clayton's parents: Raburn Stedman Rust (1862-1933), a traveling preacher, and his wife Rachel (1862-1952), who went by her middle name Ella. It's likely that Raburn helped plan the Pacific Palisades, which was founded as a Methodist commune in 1922, but his involvement is unclear because his brother Albert Rust (1866-1954) had two sons, Raburn Ross Rust (1904-1991) and Noel Rust (1905-1977), who were also in the Pacific Palisades Association.

Clayton's parents lived in his old beach house. When they moved to Arcadia, CA in 1928, they passed the house on to Ina's sister Mary Kays (1899-1973), her husband Carl (1895-1982), and their children Carl Jr. (1921-1999) and Marilyn (1924-2002).

The Rusts' property was buried by fill dirt from the bridge construction in 1933. To save their house, they moved it half a mile up the canyon to Brookside. The Kays may have faced the same problem because they also moved to Brookside.

More relatives moved nearby or were already living there.

Albert Rust's daughter Cleo (1898-1952), her husband Fred

Wendill (1892-1949), and their daughter Avis (1922-1992) lived across the creek from the Rusts.

Senea Lou Barnes's daughter Toy (1897-2006), her husband Clyde McClellan (1894-1973), and their daughter Marvelle (1923-2012) had a vacation home there. Three of Senea's children lived to be over 100, and Toy had seen three centuries by the time she died at 109.

Ina's father Josiah moved to Shady Lane in the 1920s, where he kept cows in a large field. After the 1938 flood, the Topanga road was rebuilt over his property, and he moved back to Van Nuys.

The Rusts were friends with two other Shady Lane families.

Frank (b.1892) and Ruby Porter (b.1891) taught "Topanga Beach Bible School" on Sundays to the Rusts' daughter Thais (1925-2021).

Joseph Harward (b.1886), a carpenter who lived with his wife Odessa (b.1888), finished building the interior of the Rusts' house after it was moved to Brookside.

During the 1938 Topanga fire, Thais's bedroom on the second floor burned. Clayton single-handedly saved the rest of the house by pouring buckets of water from his fishpond onto the roof. Flames burned a handkerchief in his back pocket, but he somehow escaped injury. In the garage was a propane tank that could have exploded at any moment.

Lower Topanga's location, on the borderline between city and county land, often caused odd responses. In this case, fire trucks parked on the boulevard but wouldn't enter the neighborhood. This inaction contributed to the large number of homes that burned there. The Kays were among the unfortunates, but they were able to rebuild with lumber and supplies donated by The Red Cross. Amazingly, the next day Ina cooked everyone a Thanksgiving dinner.

Around this time, a fire station was built at the Topanga intersection, on a lot formerly occupied by the office of Los Angeles Athletic Club property manager Guy Wade (1880-1979). Wade's office was lifted up and added onto the roof. The fire station later became part of the Malibu Feed Bin.

Guy, his wife Elsie (1877-1937), and daughter Elizabeth (1904-2000) had a cottage at Brookside. He and Clayton were friends, and took hunting and fishing trips together in the Sierra Nevada Mountains.

In 1944, Clayton and Ina divorced. Clayton stayed in Lower Topanga, while Ina took wartime jobs at Garrett AiResearch and Douglas Aircraft in the city. She continued to work in aerospace after the war.

CHAPTER 25

Early Surfers

In 2005, former *Topanga Messenger* editor Susan Chasen and I interviewed the Rusts' daughter Thais (1925-2021) about growing up in Lower Topanga. Thais's memories, many of which we published in the newspaper and re-published in *The Topanga Story*, presented a vision of our hometown so unfamiliar that it astonished us.

One of Thais's earliest memories was watching the enormous German Graf Zeppelin fly by Topanga Beach on its 1929 trip around the world. A few years later, the zeppelin would become a symbol of Nazi propaganda and carry the swastika.

Thais also remembered the gambling ships of the 1930s, which would sometimes anchor off Topanga. They had to stay three miles from the coast to avoid US laws.

Holiday fun was had at the annual "Webster Christmas Party for the Children of Malibu," a 20-year tradition at John L. Webster's Malibu Courthouse that started in 1932, and drew hundreds.

A simpler ritual was collecting honey with painter Laura Way Mathiesen (1876-1966), who kept her bees in a side canyon that doubled as a shooting range for the police.

Thais's favorite memories were of spending whole summers on the beach with her cousin Marilyn Kays (1924-2002), and neighbors Dick Carhart and Ida Lee Carrillo (1924-1948).

> We were at the beach probably from eight or nine in the morn-

> ing till five or six at night. It didn't matter how large the waves were, we just had fun....
>
> One day, Marilyn and I went with Ida Lee and her dad to the beach. The three of us got out beyond the waves, not knowing that there was a strong riptide. When we couldn't get back to shore, Ottie called the Santa Monica lifeguards to rescue us. We were picked up just before Sunset Blvd. We were having a great time but Ida Lee's dad was frantic.

Ida Lee was the daughter of Octavio "Ottie" (1889-1980) and Bessie Carrillo (1889-1980), the niece of actor Leo Carrillo (1880-1961), and a descendant of one of California's oldest Spanish families.

Other swimming options were the bathhouse of Alfred Patterson Stewart, rebuilt after the 1926 fire and nicknamed The Plunge, and the private swimming pool of actor/Olympian Johnny Weissmuller (1904-1984) at Las Tunas Beach, where the neighborhood kids liked to jump in from the balcony.

Weissmuller was probably a vacation renter of actress Natalie Talmadge (1896-1969), who lived there with her sons Joseph "James" (1922-2007) and Robert "Bob" (1924-2009). She legally changed their surnames to Talmadge to avoid being reminded of her famous ex-husband Buster Keaton (1895-1966).

In the early 1940s, actors David Niven (1910-1983) and Errol Flynn (1909-1959) took over the house, with Bing Crosby (1903-1977) and Paulette Goddard (1910-1990) living on either side. In the mid-1940s, it became the Las Tunas Isle Motel. Today it's a private residence at 18904 PCH.

After high school, Thais became engaged to Bob Talmadge, but they broke up before the wedding. During World War II, she spent Friday nights scanning the sky for enemy planes from a lookout tower that was across the street from today's Getty Villa.

In the early 1950s, she was briefly married to a second beach resident, Dave Sykes (1926-2009).

However, a third man from the beach was destined to become her life partner, and surprisingly it was Dave's younger brother, John "Jack" Sykes (1935-2017), whom she married in 1956.

Jack, Dave, and their sister Beverly (1930-2001) were the children of Sherman (1895-1986) and Gladys Sykes (1897-1987), who owned a bar called The Glen, in Beverly Glen. It had a reputation for being tough, and Sherman carried a gun that he would sometimes leave out on the family table. Their house had a gangplank that led onto the sand. When it was pulled up, it covered the door to keep big waves from splashing in.

Chasen and I interviewed Jack simultaneously, and he shared vivid memories of what Topanga Beach was like during World War II.

By then, the gambling ships had been outlawed, but the Air Force kept an abandoned one off Topanga for target practice. The hills along the coast were full of artillery. It was a common sight to see 100 army vehicles at a time driving down the highway in convoy. At night, drivers kept their headlights off, and a Blackout Warden fined houses where light was visible. One night, a tank came to investigate a fishing boat that shouldn't have been there.

The Coast Guard had a headquarters at Sunset Blvd., and patrolled the coast on foot every evening, passing by Topanga Beach with bayonets and German Shepherds. Sometimes the army closed the beach to play war games.

Machine gun nests were placed on dirt mounds on either side of the lagoon. One was in front of Jack's house.

> They dug a big hole in the sand, and had soldiers in there. I would bring them cookies from our house, and my dad got so mad at me. I was taking all our stuff out for these guys to eat.

Contrasting with the wartime grittiness was the glamour of Jack's celebrity neighbors, like actresses Greta Garbo (1905-1990), with whom he took walks, and Shirley Temple (1928-2014), who occasionally asked his dad for a ride to town.

Jack was also surrounded by icons of early California surfing, which included his brother.

> [Dave] Sykes was the best surfer I had seen at that time because he lived there and surfed all day, every day. He could just glide and glide.
>
> —Joe Quigg, "The Archivist: Turning Points" *The Surfer's Journal*, 2017-09-19

> Topanga dweller Sykes' finely honed speed lines and turning were years in advance of others. Sykes delighted in perfect planing surfaces and placed 15 layers of hand rubbed lacquer over his boards creating a hard shelled outer surface many years before the discovery of fiberglass and resin.
>
> —Craig Stecyk, *The Surfer's Journal*

The Malibu Point was first surfed in September 1927, when it was still a private ranch, by Tom Blake (1902-1994) and Sam Reid (1905-1978). We don't know who first surfed Topanga, but it would make sense for Tom and Sam to have tried it before Malibu. Reid is often quoted as saying that "there were only six surfboards in the entire United States" when he graduated from Santa Monica High School in the early 1920s.

Although Reid's count was meant more to give an impression, two of those "six" surfboards belonged to brothers John E. O. (1915-1990) and Jim Larronde (1917-1989), whose parents had them engraved with the boys' initials in Hawaii and shipped to their Topanga Beach vacation house in 1921 (John's redwood board is now in the Museum of Ventura County). In the late 1930s, a transition balsa-redwood surfboard was called the Larronde Model. In the late 1940s, John made a 16-minute home surf movie, popularly known as *Sweet Sixteen*, of trips he took between Malibu and Santa Barbara.

Their father Pedro Larronde (1875-1922) supposedly built their beach house in 1917, just after the prison camp closed. He may have been given this privilege because his brother John M. (1878-1954) was an executive of the Title Insurance and Trust Company.

Or it may have happened because their grandfather Pierre (1826-1896) had been the legal guardian of Deputy Sheriff Eugene Biscailuz's uncle William (1864-1943), who was also of Basque ancestry.

Pedro was an executive of the Franco-American Baking Company, and a member of the Los Angeles Athletic Club. For some reason, his wife Gladys (1883-1950) was forced to move their beach house across the street to Old Malibu Road when the LAAC took ownership in the mid-1920s.

The Larronde house became known as the Three J's Inn, after the boys and their sister Juanita (1912-2004). It was bulldozed in the mid-2000s, along with the Rust house and the rest of Lower Topanga, after State Parks took ownership.

Other early Topanga Beach surfers were Ted Berkeley (1912-1997), Chuck Spurgin (1916-1996), Bob Simmons (1919-1954), Don James (1921-1996), Ed Fearon (b.1921), Jack Quigg (b.1922), the Talmadge brothers, Warren Miller (1924-2018), half-brothers Jerry Hanes (b.1924) and Bobby Jacks (1927-1987), Mike Roberts (1925-2014), Dick Hunt (1926-1967), brothers Dave (1928-2015) and Roger Sweet (b.1930), brothers Ted (1928-1951) and Fred Harrison (b.1931), Howard Terrill (1929-2019), Matt Kivlin (1929-2014), and twin brothers Corny (1930-2011) and Peter Cole (1930-2022).

More than just a random surf pack, this group is actually noted for evolving the sport with their skill, precociousness, and other contributions.

Don James was California's first dedicated surf photographer.

Bob Simmons and Dave Sweet were influential shapers.

Warren Miller was an early surf filmmaker, then transitioned to ski filming, a passion which he traced back to a freak snowstorm at Topanga Beach.

> Many people and businesses change forever because of a simple event. Mine changed on the beach at Topanga Canyon in 1929. It had snowed about an inch the night before and as I walked barefooted in ankle-deep warm ocean water, I stepped out onto the snow and a kind of visceral feeling happened that to this day is impossible for me to explain.
>
> —"Nostalgia," *Idaho Mountain Express*, 2010-01-22

(No snow was reported in 1929. Miller could be remembering the snows that fell in the winter of 1931-32.)

Matt Kivlin was considered to be the best California surfer of his generation, and Kathy "Gidget" Kohner (b.1941) caught her first wave on his board, which led to an explosion in surfing's popularity.

Peter Cole moved to Hawaii to become a big-wave rider, and his brother Corny became the art director of Topanga Beach's own *Surf Guide* magazine.

World War II interrupted the lives of many of these young surfers, but offered unexpected opportunities for the Rust women. Thais followed her mom into the aerospace field, getting her first job at Douglas Aircraft. She went on to work at the RAND Corporation and the Planning Research Corporation.

Jack was too young to fight in World War II, but chose a military career anyway when he came of age. He then worked as a plumber, and eventually started his own company.

Jack and Thais raised two daughters, Lori (b.1958) and Lisa (1961-2018), and retired in Orange, CA.

Lower Topanga Trivia

Early fires

1911-11-18	A brush fire likely burned the chain gang stockade
1923-07-04	A brush fire started at the Fire Rodeo
1926-01-03	A house fire burned 10 beach cabins and a bathhouse
1938-11-23	A brush fire burned Elkhorn Camp and nearly 50 homes

Early floods/storms

1905-03-13	Arch Rock was damaged
1906-03-23	Arch Rock collapsed
1916-01	Elkhorn Camp was flooded
1926-02	Waves swept away 14 beach houses and a fish market
1927-02-04	Waves swept away 5 beach houses
1929 ('31-32?)	A freak snowstorm hit the beach
1938-03-01	The Topanga road washed out
1941-02-20	John Foundoukos saved the Morgan family with his boat

Early films

The Treasure Hunters, 1910. Status unknown. Location: near the former Arch Rock. A young man sails to an island in search of treasure.

Crossing the American Prairies in the Early Fifties, 1911. Unreleased. Director: D. W. Griffith. Stars: Myrtle Dennison, Dell Henderson, W. Chrystie Miller. Location: the Topanga Lagoon. Indians ambush a wagon train. See p. 128.

A Chance Shot, 1911. Status unknown. Director: Pat Hartigan. Star: Ruth Roland. Location: the Topanga Beach Native American mound. A Native binds a White woman to a tree when she doesn't return his love.

The Adventurer, 1917. Available. Director: Charlie Chaplin. Stars: Charlie

Chaplin, Edna Purviance, Eric Campbell. Location: the Topanga intersection. A man escapes from a prison camp. See p. 131.

Unknown Title, 1919. Location: the Topango Ranch. "…a famous English actress had to be lifted onto her pony for equestrian scenes."

A Sailor-Made Man, 1921. Available. Director: Fred C. Newmeyer. Stars: Harold Lloyd, Mildred Davis, Noah Young. Location: Las Tunas Beach. A man joins the Navy to prove himself to the girl he loves.

Thorobred, 1922; shot in 1921 with the working title *Going Some*. Status unknown. Director: George Halligan. Stars: Helen Gibson, Bob Burns, Otto Nelson. Location: the Topango Ranch. The sheriff's daughter takes over when he becomes sick.

The Lone Star Ranger; ***Hell's Hole***; ***The Grail***; or ***Mile-a-Minute Romeo***, 1923. Lost. Star: Tom Mix; Buck Jones; Dustin Farnum; or Tom Mix. Location: the Topango Ranch. Actor A. M. Fenton broke his shoulder while making one of these films.

Champion, 1949. Available. Director: Mark Robson. Stars: Kirk Douglas, Arthur Kennedy, Marilyn Maxwell, Ruth Roman. Location: the Step Inn Cafe. A boxer rises to fame by betraying friends and family.

Early artworks

Unknown Title, c. 1900. Unknown painter. Allison-Claire Acker collection. Jack Rabbit Lodge. See p. 124.

Unknown Titles, 1910. Lillian Buell. Unknown collection. "She has been sketching around Santa Monica and Topanga for four months and has many of our most interesting views."

Driven Sea, 1913. Painting by George Laurence Schreiber (1862-1940). Unknown collection. "One of the largest canvasses… the ocean at the old Arch Rock."

Topanga Canyon, 1914. Théodore Gégoux (1850-1931). Unknown collection. The Topanga Lagoon.

Topanga Canyon—Mountains on the Coast, 1915. Théodore Gégoux (1850-1931). Unknown collection. The Topanga Lagoon. See p. 127.

Little Picnic in Topanga, c. 1922. Jane McDuffie Thurston (1887-1967). Pasadena Art Monkeys gallery. View of Cooper's Camp and the lagoon.

Topanga Creek, 1923. George Demont Otis (1879-1962). Unknown collection. A view looking up Topanga Canyon from the lagoon.

11 Unknown Titles, 1924. Paintings by Laura Way (1876-1966). Unknown collection. "I have so small a background of ocean experience…. I felt really bewildered at the heaving, tumbling mass."

Untitled, 1924. Print by Laura Way. Unknown collection. "…a little print experiment of mine which will give you an idea of the type of scenery we have on our way to town as the highway is right along the beach."

Marmont Studio, 1924. Print by Laura Way. Unknown collection. "...a sketch of the studio which is used as a headpiece for the invitation."

8 Unknown Titles, 1925. Paintings by Laura Way. Unknown collection. "... thumb box paintings of California beach scenes."

Green Slopes of Topanga, 1927. Painting by Laura Way. Unknown collection. No description.

The Opal Bay, 1928. Painting by Laura Way. Unknown collection. "A gorgeous sunset on Santa Monica Bay has here dyed both sky and sea with opal tinted light, filtering through the mist and partly revealing the distant land to the north."

The Silver Thread Along the Shore, 1928. Painting by Laura Way. Unknown collection. "[S]he paints the sunlight as it hits the water," "a large and excellent view of the northern end of Santa Monica Bay, in misty mood."

Marmont Studio, 1929. Painting by Laura Way. Unknown collection. "Mrs. Mathieson's little house in the moonlight is quaint and charming, and one finds many art lovers enjoying it at the gallery each day, intrigued by the atmosphere attained by values well handled."

Foothill Landscape, unknown date. Painting by George Melcher (1881-1957). Unknown collection. Topanga Creek near Brookside.

Topango Beach, circa 1930. Print by Arthur Millier (1893-1975). Barbara Kohn collection. Fishermen prepare to go out in rowboats.

Marmont Studio, 1933. Print by Laura Way. Justina Judge-Stevenson collection. "...the studio at right, and the cabin at the left, both nestling on a mountain slope with a mountain range in the background and much foliage in the foreground." See p. 147.

Trampers' Annex of the Los Angeles Athletic Club

Members who hiked to Topanga Beach, and the date of the trip

- Thomas Gibson — 1894-11-11
- H. L. Jenkins — 1894-11-11
- Phil Marx — 1894-11-11
- John S. Thayer, of the LA Wheelmen, rode a bike — 1894-11-11
- Abe Jacoby — 1895-03-17
- James Ryan, captain — 1895-03-17
- A. E. Slaught — 1895-03-17
- O. E. Smith — 1895-03-17
- T. H. Bearing, secretary-treasurer — both trips
- Isidore Marschutz, first lieutenant — both trips
- Walter McStay, president — both trips

- F. Ryder both trips
- Ed Wolfstein both trips

People on the 1910 Stanford Geology field trip

Staff

- Fatty Harry, a Japanese dishwasher boy, so "lovingly called"
- Frank the Pirate, a Japanese cook
- Robert Land (maybe)
- George Macready
- Ben Parsons
- John Roy "Billie" Pemberton, professor
- a spotted dog

Students

- Bill Arrell
- Jim Boundy
- Bill Burcham
- Weldon Crook
- Tom Haliday
- Harold Hannibal
- Joe Hook
- Knight Jordan
- Gill Lewis
- Earl Lieb
- Kid Menke
- Ducky Merrit
- Bill Nash
- Dan Nolan
- Young Packard
- Mike Peckham
- Virgil Prout
- Clayton Robbins
- Kid Small
- Sassy Taylor
- Kid Templeton
- Joe Waring
- Jim Wilde
- Caesar Young

Prisoners who escaped from the chain gang, 1914-1917

- M. L. Alconta (Alcantro?) …escaped twice
- Felipe Baritesta
- A. G. Bowler …escaped twice, recaptured
- Francisco Flores
- Juan Gonzales …recaptured
- Vera Gonzales
- J. B. Hernan …recaptured
- Domencio Hernandez …recaptured
- Mr. Houseman
- Claude Johnson …recaptured
- LeRoy Martin
- Juan Martinez …recaptured
- "Shorty" Charles Lee Quin (Quinn?) …escaped twice, recaptured
- Reyes Silva (Silvia?) …escaped twice

People commanded to appear in Los Angeles Superior Court for "The People v. Miller Cooper, A. M. Cooper, Frank Dewar" (Case 15807) on October 11, 1922

- Helen Baker
- John C. Cline, former sheriff
- John W. Crossman (Crossan?), 666 Carondelet St.
- P. E. Fowler, 3662 Griffith
- Ruth Fowler, 3662 Griffith
- Dr. Wilbur C. Gordon, 1081 East Washington St.
- Mrs. Ruby Hanley, 1368 Neuton Ave., 950 E. 41st St.
- Thomas A. Jordan, civil engineer, Washington Building, 1153 El Molino
- Henry Monroe, Topango Store
- Arthur Valentine, 1346 East 23rd St.
- Charlotte Valentine, wife, 1346 East 23rd St.
- Newton Valentine, father, 1380 Neuton Ave.
- Horace Walker, 1368 Neuton Ave., 950 E. 41st St.
- Ida Walker, 1368 Neuton Ave.

Rodeos, 1922-1924

1922/08/27	Sheriff William Traeger Rodeo
1923/06/2-3	Elks Rodeo
1923/06/24	New Bridge Rodeo
1923/07/04	Fire Rodeo
1923/09/8-9	Moose Rodeo
1923/09/30	Tom Mix Rodeo
1924/07/3-6	Bullfight Rodeo

Sheriff William Traeger Rodeo program, August 27, 1922

Events

- Calf and goat roping
- Bucking broncos
- Horse racing

Performers

- Buff Brady, champion trick rider

- Benny Crawford, champion Roman rider
- Newton House, age 10
- Hank Potts, champion bronco rider
- Dolores Steelman, age 10

Elks Rodeo program, June 2-3, 1923

EVENT 1: Cowboys' bucking contest
EVENT 2: Calf-roping contest
EVENT 3: Bull-dogging
EVENT 4: Men's pony express
EVENT 5: Girls' relay race
EVENT 6: Cowgirls' race, free-for-all, ½ mile
EVENT 7: Steer riding
EVENT 8: Chariot race, ½ mile
EVENT 9: Chuck wagon race, ½ mile
EVENT 10: Trick roping by cowboys and cowgirls
EVENT 11: Trick riding by cowboys and cowgirls
EVENT 12: Roman standing race, ¾ mile
EVENT 13: Wild cow milking contest

- George C. Flores, Director
- Alvin J. Neitz, Chairman of the Rodeo Committee

Fancy ropers and riders

- Bob Anderson, Newhall, CA
- Clarence Burgett, Newhall, CA
- Ben Corbett, Pendleton, CA
- J. Donaldson, Pawhuska, OK
- Roby Frobe, Pendleton, CA
- "Tuck" Gibson, Los Angeles, CA
- Harry Hill, Colorado Springs, CO
- Happy Holt, Pendleton, OR
- Sam Howe, Bakersfield, CA
- Roy Jones, Los Angeles, CA
- Scoop Martin, Pendleton, OR
- Dorothy Morrell, Cheyenne, WY
- "Skeeter Bill" Robbins, Cheyenne, WY
- Miguel Severas, Sonora, Mexico

Other performers

- Bob Arickson, Red Bluffs, CA
- Al Brassfield, Casper, WY
- Hippy Burmeister, Los Angeles, CA
- Perry Ivory, Alturas, CA
- Skeet Johnson, Gila Bend, AZ
- Cliff Lyons, Cheyenne, WY
- "Wild Cat" McCarty, Bosman, MT
- Don McDonald, Calgary, Canada
- Calgary Jack McDonald, Calgary, Canada
- Frank Smith, Miles City, MT
- Clarence Sovern, Los Angeles, CA
- Johnny Sutton, Pendleton, OR

Famous imported bucking horses

- Bald Harnett
- Blue Blazes
- Bone Breaker
- Carrie Nation
- Clown
- Happy Canyon
- Laddie Boy
- Peaceful Henry
- Pow Wow
- Mascot
- Motor Cop
- Rocking Chair
- Steamboat

Judges

- Buck Jones

New Bridge Rodeo program, June 24, 1923

- Maverick race
- Cowgirls' free-for-all race
- Pony express
- Cow pony flat race
- Trick riding
- Roman race
- Cowboy quick-change race
- Bull-dogging
- Cowboy relay
- Wild horse race
- Steer riding
- Calf roping
- Trick roping
- Chariot race
- Riding of bucking horses

Cowboys, mostly from Los Angeles

- H. Bowman
- Al Brassfield
- Milton Carter
- Archie Cooper
- Ben Corbett
- Tex Grove
- Noy Henry
- Jim Hogan
- Felix Luttrell
- J. A. MacDonald
- Gene McCay
- Clarence Pittman (Ditman?)
- Slim Riley
- Jim Shannon
- Clarence Sovern
- "Whitey" Sovern
- Hank Steelman

Cowgirls, all from Los Angeles

- Miss M. Carlson
- Helen Gibson
- Marrietta Gregory
- Miss M. Steelman
- Grace Teed

Preceding the rodeo

- Dancing girls
- Carl McStay, Southern California Automobile Club, speaker
- William H. Carter, State Highway Commission, speaker
- R. F. McClellan, LA Board of County Supervisors, speaker

Music

- The American Legion Band of Hollywood
- Miss Hazel Devere, Los Angeles, CA

Judges

- Ed Bowman
- Art Manning
- Zibe Morse

Moose Rodeo program, September 8-9, 1923

- Men's cowboy race
- Flag race
- Chuck wagon race
- Roman race
- Bucking steers
- Calf-roping
- Cowgirls' race

Calf-ropers

- Siciala Salinas, Topango Ranch
- Miguel Severas, Sonora, Mexico
- Henry Wertz Jr., Globe Mills, CA
- Henry Wertz Sr., Globe Mills, CA

Stunt riders

- Edythe Cooper, Echo Park, CA
- Myrtle Gibbins, Shelby, MT

Other events

- Horse races for men and women
- Races for fat men, girls, and boys
- A greased-pig free-for-all
- A badger fight at midnight
- Tug-of-war
- A greased-pole climb
- Mack Sennett's bathing girls' contest/parade
- The Queen of the Moose contest
- The triumphal procession of the Queen in her chariot

Music

- The American Legion Band of Hollywood
- The Moose Orchestra

Tom Mix Rodeo program, September 30, 1923

Performers

- Edythe Cooper won the flat quarter-mile race
- Justice John L. Fleming
- Walter Lucore
- Deputy Sheriff Art Manning
- Tom Mix rode Tony the Wonder Horse
- Stub Musselman
- Clarence Sovern rode Chain Lightning
- Jonesy Willett

Judges

- Justice Charles S. Crail
- Tom Mix
- Justice John W. Summerfield

Music

- The American Legion Band of Hollywood
- Boy Scouts band, led by Philip Memoli

People arrested on August 16, 1925 for selling liquor at the Rustle Inn

- Charles P. Flood
- Deputy Sheriff William Edward Harris, proprietor
- Mrs. Ruth Santee
- Theodore P. "Teddy" Santee, her son
- Ben Shuff (M. Shubb? Dr. Shauff?)
- Deputy Fire Warden H. D. Smith, proprietor
- John W. Yeuk

Victims of the beach house fire on January 3, 1926

The fire started in the empty cabin of D. B. Stewart and spread in both directions.

On one side, it burned the house of Mr. Patelane, the bathhouse of Alfred Patterson Stewart, and a dance pavilion (partially).

On the other side, it burned the houses of dentist Dr. Shauff, Ivon Parker, his brother Claude I. Parker (of Parker Mesa), Deputy Sheriff George Saunders, Ross Eville, J. C. Casey, Mr. Hawks, and Mr. Snodgrass, whose house was torn down to prevent further progress.

The only cabins occupied where those of Ivon, Saunders, Eville and Snodgrass. They rushed out into the cold night "very scantily clad."

Because of a lack of water, firemen used axes and pinch bars.

Photo Gallery

Arch Rock, c. 1880 *University of Southern California Libraries / California Historical Society*

Topanga pioneers celebrate the opening of the canyon road in 1898. Ben Failor checks on the horses. Columbus Cheney embraces wife Lucy. Lucy Greenleaf embraces husband Charles. Mary Failor and Tillie Manners are behind them. Mrs. Edwin Erdman sits next to Mort Allen. Eddie Erdman, 3, is behind them. *Edwin Erdman / Topanga Historical Society*

***Unknown Title (Jack Rabbit Lodge)*, unknown painter, early 1900s** *Acker Archive*

Topanga Lagoon, 1900 *Santa Monica Public Library*

Jack Rabbit Lodge and a long barn, c. 1910 *Acker Archive*

Jack Rabbit Lodge, c. 1910 *Topanga Historical Society*

W. W. Coolbaugh, amateur archaeologist
Los Angeles Times, 1911-02-05

Artifacts found by Coolbaugh
Los Angeles Times, 1911-01-15

Detail from *Topanga Canyon—Mountains on the Coast* by Théodore Gégoux, after Coolbaugh's home Jack Rabbit Lodge was burned down, 1915 *unknown*

Stanford Geological Society, 1909. J. R. Pemberton, standing fourth from left, led a similar group that excavated a burial mound at Topanga Beach in 1910. *Stanford Yearbook*

D. W. Griffith directed *Crossing the American Prairies in the Early Fifties* from the saddle of a cream-colored horse. He included 200 cowboys from nearby ranches, 50 women and children, 120 horses, and 11 prairie schooners.
Los Angeles Times, 1911-05-15

Topanga Canyon road under construction, c. 1913 *Randy Young Collection*

Topanga pioneer Dolores Trujillo, probably in the left front seat, drives road-building equipment back to the beach, c. 1913 *Topanga Historical Society*

The prison camp of the chain gang, c. 1913 *Theresa Sletton / Huntington Library*

Charlie Chaplin escapes from the prison camp in *The Adventurer*, 1917

Cooper's Camp, early 1920s *H. F. Rile / Santa Monica Public Library*

The dance pavilion, c. 1921 *unknown*

Cooper's Camp, "Beach cabins spring up like magic," c. 1921 *Acker Archive*

Elkhorn Camp, a mile and a half from the beach, date unknown *Acker Archive*

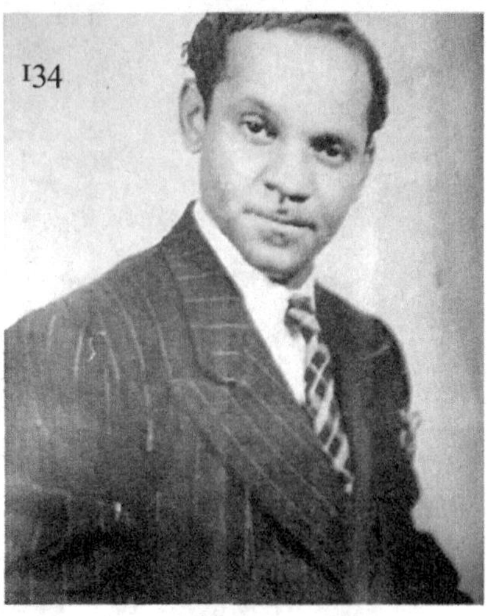

Arthur Valentine Jr. *Valentine Family*

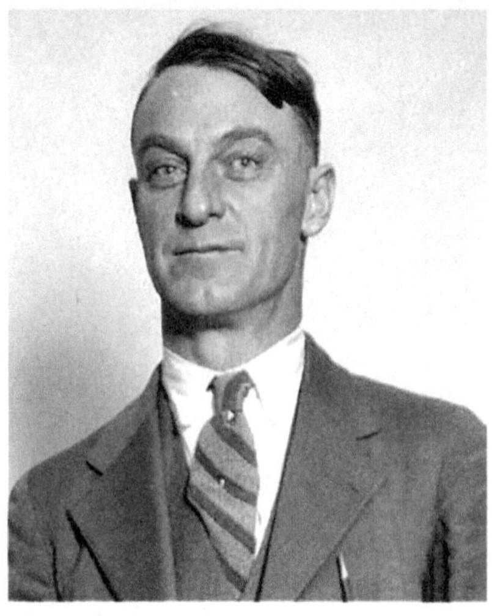

Deputy Sheriff Frank DeWar *unknown*

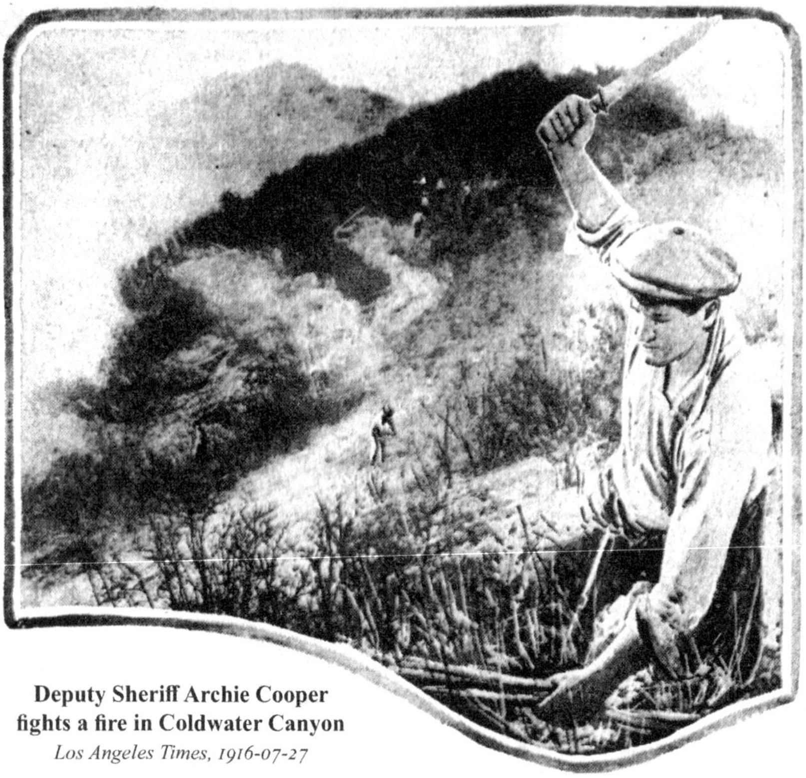

Deputy Sheriff Archie Cooper fights a fire in Coldwater Canyon
Los Angeles Times, 1916-07-27

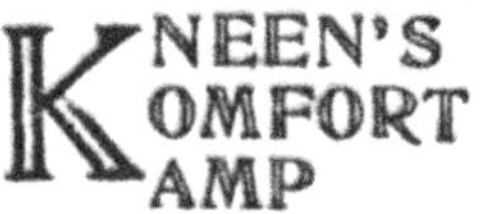

KNEEN'S KOMFORT KAMP TOPANGA An hour's ride from heart of Los Angeles, on main boulevard. Housekeeping tents, $6 per week—write for particulars and reservations. Kneen's Kamp, Topanga, Cal.

Kneen's Kamp, nearby, advertised with the initials KKK *Los Angeles Times 1919-07-09*

Actress Helen Gibson in *The Black Horse Bandit*, 1919 *Larry Telles Collection*

Gibson did stunts in *The Hazards of Helen*, 1914–17 *Margaret Herrick Library Collection*

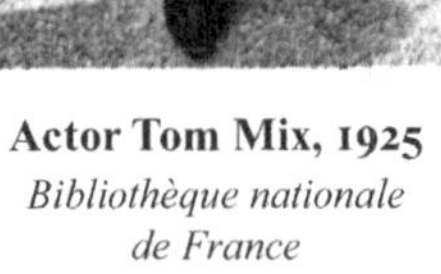

Actor Tom Mix, 1925
Bibliothèque nationale de France

Sam "Buffalo" Smith
Los Angeles Times 1923-09-06

"Tuck" Gibson rides Steamboat in The Rodeo Grounds
Santa Monica E. Outlook, 1923-05-30

A cowboy rides a bucking steer in The Rodeo Grounds, c. 1923 *Acker Archive*

Edythe Cooper rides a trick pony on the Topango Ranch *Illustrated Daily News, 1923-09-05*

EVERYTHING is all set for the Elks' Round-up at Topanga Beach which opens at eleven o'clock Saturday morning with a big free picnic for the orphans of Santa Monica Bay.

From eleven till two the children will be entertained with all kinds of out door sports and during the noon hour a big free lunch will be served.

The wild west show starts at two o'clock and will be repeated at the same time Sunday afternoon. Famous riders and ropers from Wyoming, Montana, Arizona and Oregon

Skeet Johnson practices in The Rodeo Grounds *Los Angeles Record, 1923-06-01*

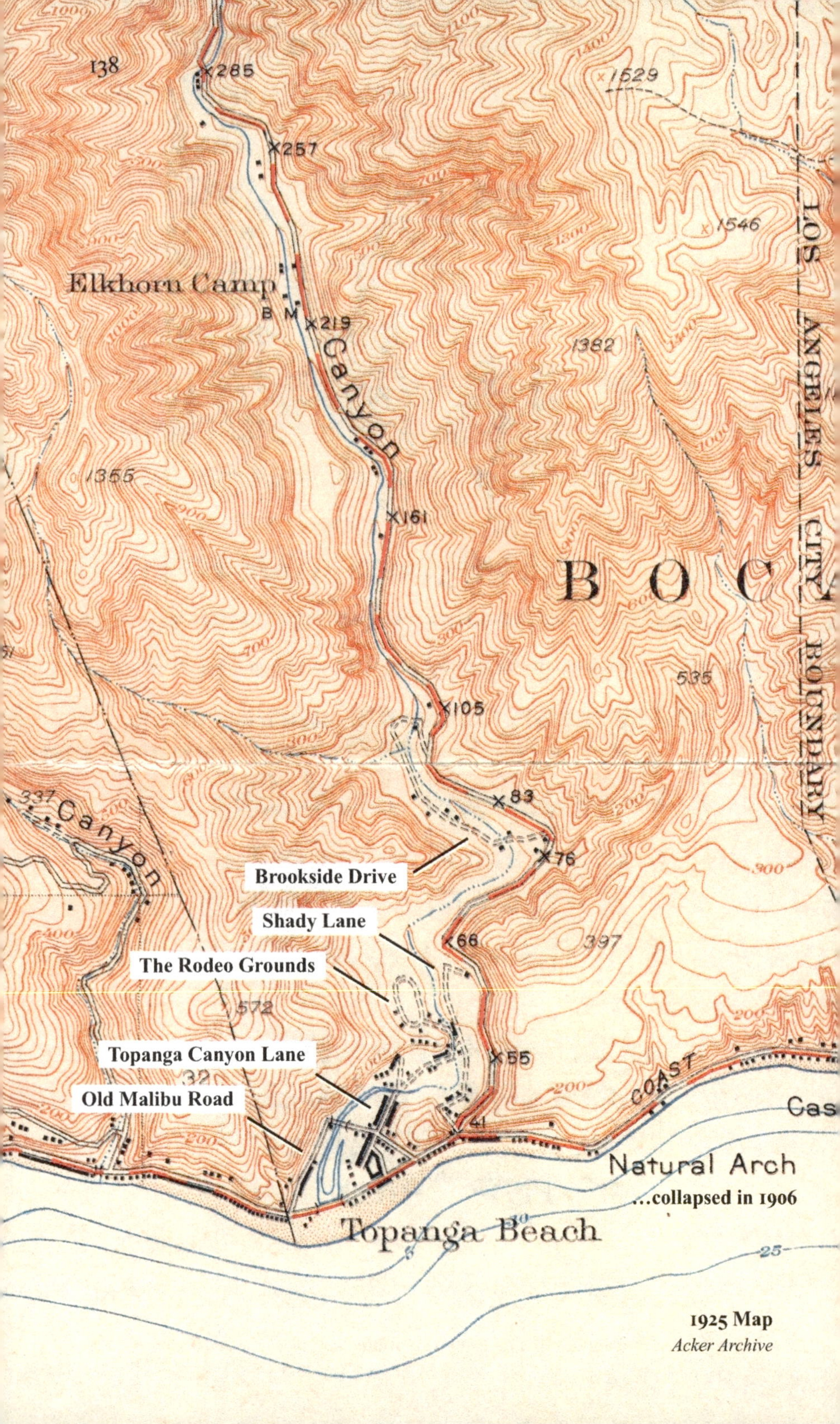

Natural Arch ...collapsed in 1906

1925 Map
Acker Archive

Topanga Beach, 1924, the year of Sam Rizzio's poison ceremony *Los Angeles Public Library*

May Otis Blackburn and Ruth Wieland:
The Great Eleven cult leaders, 1929

Sam Rizzio and Ruth Wieland, 1924
Los Angeles Times

Cooper's Camp, 1926, after most of the beach houses were destroyed by waves and fire

The Rodeo Grounds on the Topango Ranch *University of California Los Angeles Libraries*

Clayton Rust's gas station at the Topanga intersection, c. 1920 *Sykes Family Collection*

Corner fruit and vegetable stand, 1922 *University of California Los Angeles Libraries*

Title Insurance and Trust Company office with store below, 1928 *Topanga Historical Society*

Gas station, Los Angeles Athletic Club office, Potter's Store, 1933 *Sykes Family Collection*

Ina, Clayton, Rust's Barbecue, c. 1930 *Sykes Family*

Thais Rust, John Foundoukos, c. 1928 *Sykes Family*

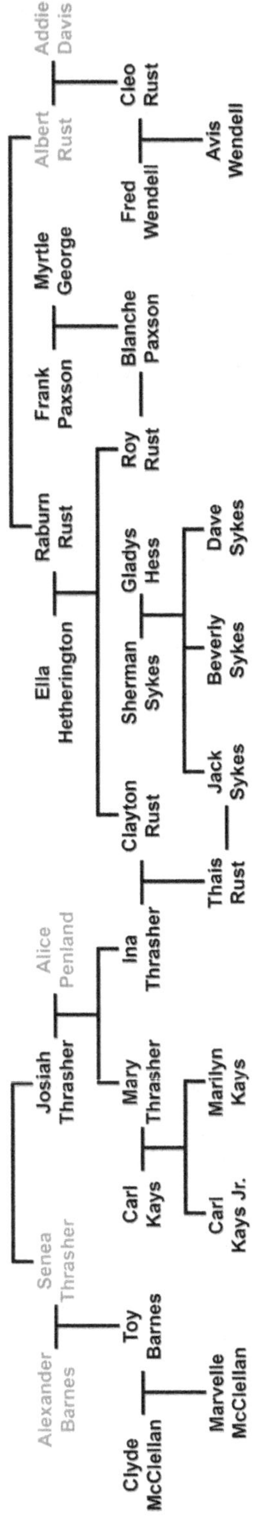

Rust-Thrasher Family members who lived/worked at Topanga Beach. Those who did not are either omitted or listed in gray.

The Rust Family, c. 1928. FRONT: Ellen Rust Penland, Joanne Simmons, Thais Rust, Ray and Leon Simmons, Ella Rust, Avis Wendill, Fern Rust, Raburn Stedman Rust. MIDDLE: Clayton Rust, Roy Rust, Claude Simmons, Edythe Rust, Fleta Rust, unknown, Ina Rust, Mildred Rust (?). BACK: Frank (or Joe?) Rust, Blanche Rust, Art Rust, Archie Rust, Ernest Rust. *Sykes Family*

Topanga Beach kids at the Rusts' house, c. 1930. FRONT: Edna Mae Spence, Marilyn Burns, Bill Hoskins, Joyce Wiard, Mary Miller, Thais Rust, unknown, unknown. MIDDLE: unknown, Marvelle McClellan, Avis Wendill, unknown, Betty Miller, Marilyn Kays, unknown. BACK: Frank Rust, Gil Hoskins, Warren Miller, Carl Kays Jr., unknown, Teddy Ranberg, Franklin Pierce. *Sykes Family*

The beach bathhouse and the Rustle Inn restaurant, c. 1926 *Acker Archive*

The Rusts' house at left behind the Auto Court, late 1920s *Acker Archive*

Laura Way, painter
Justina Judge-Stevenson Collection

Laura's print of her Marmont Studio, 1933
Justina Judge-Stevenson Collection

Laura W. Mathiesen 1933.

Marmont Studio

Florence, William, and Edna Mae Spence with Skippy the dog at Spence's Cabins, 1936
Beverly Spence Kirkpatrick Collection

Spence's Cabins, a motel on Topanga Lane, 1930s *Beverly Spence Kirkpatrick Collection*

ABOVE: Sign on the coast highway, 1930s

LEFT: Thomas Spence, c. 1930

BELOW: Thomas's boat "Popeye," 1931

Beverly Spence Kirkpatrick Collection

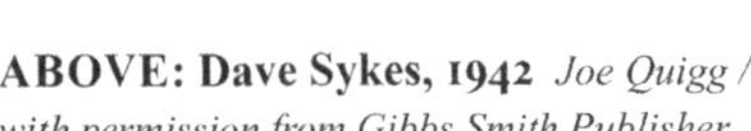

ABOVE: Dave Sykes, 1942 *Joe Quigg / with permission from Gibbs Smith Publisher*

TOP RIGHT:
Jerry Hanes, Bobby Jacks, Bob Talmadge, c. 1942 *Sykes Family Collection*

BOTTOM: Warren Miller with his board "Warnie," c. 1947 *Warren Miller*

Ed Fearon, Don James, and Jack Quigg took this photo in front of their Topanga Beach house on the day that Pearl Harbor was attacked, December 7, 1941. *Don James*

Dave Sweet, circa 1949, became an influential surfboard shaper *Joe Quigg*

www.BrassTacksPress.com

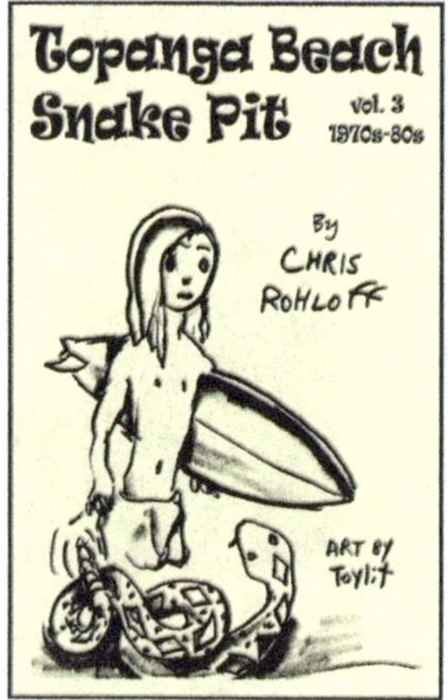

Index

Made in the USA
Coppell, TX
09 February 2026

70658509R00089